MOSAIC KNITTING

MODERN GEOMETRIC
ACCESSORIES FOR YOU
AND YOUR HOME

Workshop

ASHLEIGH WEMPE

DAVID & CHARLES

www.davidandcharles.com

Contents

Introduction

I've had the insatiable need to always have a knitting project on my needles ever since I picked up yarn for the first time as a high schooler. When a dear family friend showed me the basics of knitting and introduced me to a yarn store - I was absolutely hooked - to borrow a crochet term! I still feel that initial sense of awe when observing the beautiful colors of yarn fibers in my own creations or someone else's. It never gets old!

Knitting is my stress relief. It's been my source of calm through life's major events. Like an encouraging friend, it got me through college exam week. It was a constructive form of procrastination while writing my master's thesis, and it kept me awake while working night shifts in the Air Force. I even brought a half-knit shawl to the hospital when my first-born daughter decided it was time to make her worldly debut. Full disclosure, I didn't knit a single stitch on the Labor and Delivery Ward but the 'intent' to knit somehow relaxed me as a brand new momma.

If you're like me, this might sound familiar: For the first few years of knitting life, my loved ones received a simple scarf and chunky, misshapen hat full of dropped stitches. Gift recipients politely smiled and the items never again saw the light of day.

It's a knitter's rite-of-passage to finally have a family member, or close friend, cherish one of their works-of-art enough to proudly adorn it publicly. Non-knitters just don't know the thrill of casting on a project, trying out a new technique, and then giving away labors of love to those who appreciate it!

After several years of knitting, I took the plunge and started designing my own patterns. The possibilities of knitwear design prove endless and there is always something new to learn. I love playing with bright colors, bold geometric shapes, and simple stitches (I love to binge #knitflix as much as the next knitter by the way).

Mosaic knitting can look complex at first, but after learning the basic technique, it proves quite easy and accessible to adventurous beginners. If you can knit, purl, slip a stitch or two, and create two-row stripes, you have all the requisite skills to knit mosaic colorwork! I've relished the challenge of showcasing mosaic knitting in a book, capturing for you a style rich in beautiful modern motifs. It has been an unexpected and delightful journey to write this book.

With this book, you, the knitter, have agreed to try something new. Take my ideas and run wild with them! Use the advice and blank chart I have provided in Designing Your Own Motifs to create your own motifs. All you need to get started is a set of needles, two colors of yarn, and a bit of gumption. You can do this! Remember, please share your works of art on social media by using #mosaicknittingworkshop. Witnessing what you create is my favorite part of being a designer! You inspire me.

Love, Ashleigh

What is Mosaic Knitting?

Move over Fair Isle and intarsia because it's time for mosaic knitting to shine!

I had been knitting for over a decade before I discovered my love affair with mosaic knitting. With Fair Isle and intarsia you have to manage multiple colors at a time, long floats, and sometimes even little bobbins of yarn. There is none of that with mosaic patterns! Mosaic knitting is created using just one color at a time making it a fantastic introduction to colorwork for beginners. It's a colorwork paradise!

If you've worked stripes in two colors, you can work mosaic knitting (you might see it sometimes called slip stitch knitting).

In a nutshell, mosaic patterns are created by using one color for two rows and slipping stitches from the row below, and then switching to the other colors for two rows, slipping stitches from the previous row.

Mosaic knitting can be worked flat or in the round, and you can use either stockinette stitch, garter stitch, or a combination of the two to create completely different fabrics.

You will find that this book sticks to knitting flat with minimal shaping to make the technique accessible to most beginner knitters (although a few of the patterns contain fun, completely optional additions, like fringe and tassels, if you grow bold and want to try out something a bit more adventurous!).

The term "mosaic knitting" was originally coined by Barbara G. Walker in the late 1960s. Simple slipped stitches had been used before, but she took them to a whole new level! Her groundbreaking book, *Mosaic Knitting*, contains hundreds of mosaic patterns, and provides endless possibilities for creating your own designs. Her beautiful motifs are the inspiration behind many of the projects you will find in this book.

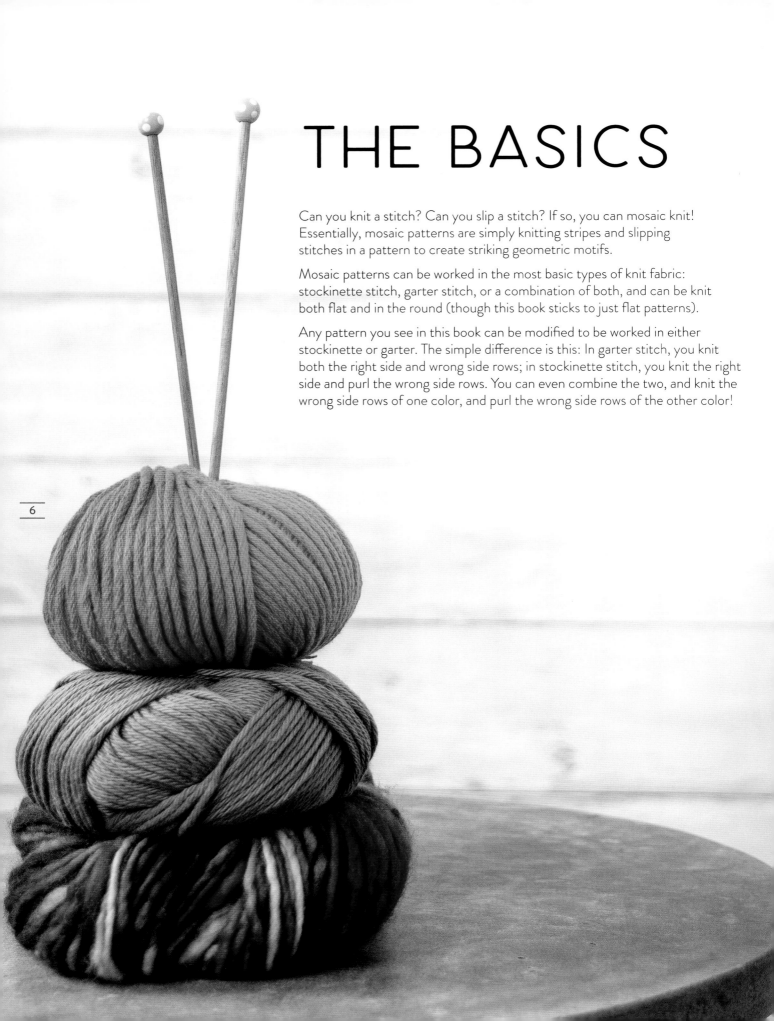

THE BASICS

Can you knit a stitch? Can you slip a stitch? If so, you can mosaic knit! Essentially, mosaic patterns are simply knitting stripes and slipping stitches in a pattern to create striking geometric motifs.

Mosaic patterns can be worked in the most basic types of knit fabric: stockinette stitch, garter stitch, or a combination of both, and can be knit both flat and in the round (though this book sticks to just flat patterns).

Any pattern you see in this book can be modified to be worked in either stockinette or garter. The simple difference is this: In garter stitch, you knit both the right side and wrong side rows; in stockinette stitch, you knit the right side and purl the wrong side rows. You can even combine the two, and knit the wrong side rows of one color, and purl the wrong side rows of the other color!

Getting Started

Are you ready to get this knitting party started? I sure am! Mosaic knitting is far easier than it appears, but I'll start by guiding you through a few key ideas that will help ensure your knitting experience is a success (I've included a lot of pictures if you happen to be a visual learner like me).

STRIPES, STRIPES, AND MORE STRIPES!

Every color in mosaic patterns is used for two rows at a time (a right side row followed by a wrong side row). The other color hangs free at the beginning of the right side row – it isn't touched until the two rows in the first color are finished. When changing to the other color, simply finish a wrong side row, turn the work so the right side faces you, drop the color that you were working with, and then pick up the next color from behind the first color and carry the yarn up the side. You will always change colors after a wrong side row when working mosaic patterns. I like to call the color that you are working your stripes with the "active" color while the color that is hanging out at the beginning of the right side row is the "inactive" color.

THE HUMBLE SLIPPED STITCH

To achieve the beautiful geometric mosaic patterns, you will knit two-row stripes as stated above, and slip certain stitches – stitches are ALWAYS slipped purlwise (on both the right and wrong side of the work). When a stitch is slipped, the working yarn is always held to the wrong side of the work – if you're working a right side row, every stitch is slipped purlwise with the yarn held in the back, and if you're working a wrong side row, every stitch is slipped purlwise with the yarn held in the front.

Like most colorwork, mosaic motifs aren't reversible, the wrong side is very obviously the back side of the fabric. Rather, the wrong side more closely resembles two-row stripes with small floats as seen in the image below.

CASTING ON AND CASTING OFF

You'll find throughout the book that I recommend a long tail cast on and either a knitted cast off or an Icelandic cast off. But, remember, recommendations are just that, recommendations! If you prefer a different cast on or cast off, go for it!

A long tail cast on is a versatile cast on technique that many beginner knitters start with as they learn to knit and purl; the first row on a long tail cast on is traditionally a wrong side row, but feel free to make it a right side row if you like how it looks (it's totally up to you).

In terms of casting off, a knitted cast off (sometimes called a traditional cast off) is usually the first cast off that beginner knitters learn. It creates a sturdy, neat edge. You can use a knitted cast off for any pattern in this book.

An Icelandic cast off is only slightly more complex than a knitted cast off, but I love it because it creates a very stretchy edge and pairs beautifully with garter stitch.

If any of these are unfamiliar to you, go check out the techniques section at the end of the book where I've created step-by-step instructions to help you out.

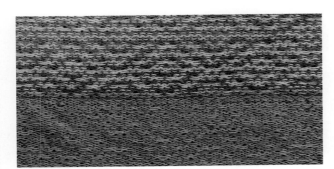

Wrong side of the Colorplay Triangle Shawl

Icelandic cast off

Knitted cast off

READING THE WRITTEN INSTRUCTIONS

Every pattern in this book is both written and charted – for more information on the charts, jump ahead to Reading the Charts. The written instructions are written like any standard pattern that has slip stitches, but will also include the color of yarn that you'll be using as your working yarn.

Let's see this in practice. Here are the written instructions for four repeats of Rows 1-4 of the Dancing Aspens Scarf (you can see what the chart looks like in Reading the Charts).

Row 1 (RS): With Mustard, k1, *sl1, k1, sl2, k3, sl1, k4; rep from * three more times, sl1, k1.

Row 2 and 4: K the same sts as k in previous row, with the active color; and slip all of the same slipped sts as slipped in previous row, wyif.

Row 3: With Steel Blue, k1, *k4, sl1, k1, sl1, k2, sl3; rep from * three more times, k2.

Broken down, here is how you'll work Rows 1 and 2:

Row 1: Start by holding the work with the right side facing you. With the colorway named Mustard, you'll knit one stitch, (slip one stitch purlwise with the yarn in back, knit one stitch, slip two stitches purlwise with the yarn in back, knit three stitches, slip one stitch purlwise with the yarn in back, knit four stitches) four times, then slip one stitch purlwise with the yarn in back, knit four stitches.

Row 2: This row will be worked just like Row 1, but in reverse. The easiest way to do this is look at your knitting – knit every stitch that you see in Mustard (the active color), and then slip every stitch with the yarn in front (or towards you) that you see in Steel Blue.

WORKING IN STOCKINETTE STITCH

Now, if I wanted to work the pattern in stockinette stitch rather than garter stitch, the instructions would stay exactly the same, except the instructions for the wrong side row instructions would read:

Rows 2 and 4 (WS): P the same sts as k in previous row, with the active color; and slip all of the same slipped sts as slipped in previous row, wyif.

That's it!

TIP

I added four edge stitches in garter stitch at the beginning and end of the row of each swatch – this helps to prevent the stockinette version from curling.

You'll find written instructions for each pattern in this book, as well as some written instructions within the charted instructions for any stockinette or garter sections that might also be included in the pattern.

Swatch in garter stitch

Swatch in stockinette stitch

CARRYING THE YARN UP THE SIDE

Whenever you knit two-row stripes (or work mosaic patterns!), you carry the yarn up the side of your knitting. But, what does that look like? You actually have a few options here.

Option A:

Let's say you just finished knitting two rows of Color A and now need to work two rows in Color B. For most of the patterns in this book, the instructions are to always knit (or purl if working a wrong side row in stockinette stitch) the first and last stitch of each row in the active color.

The most discreet way to change colors is to lift the new color from **behind** the old color to begin knitting with the new color. The result of this will be a raw edge similar to the edge of a garter stitch fabric – it will look very similar, but not exactly the same as the left hand side of your work. This small difference is hardly noticeable.

If you bring the new yarn in **front** of the old yarn, you will end up with small floats between rows on the right edge of your knitting.

Option B:

Now, if you prefer a neater edge, here is a solution that creates nearly identical edges (this edge is used in a couple of the patterns in this book).

On every right side row, lift the new color in front of the old color, then knit the first stitch through the back loop, and then slip the last stitch with the yarn held in front.

On every wrong side row, you'll knit the first stitch, and then slip the last stitch with the yarn held in front.

Note: If you decide you would like to use this technique on a pattern that uses Option A, you will want to add two stitches when casting on your work. You'll work the above instructions for the first and last stitches at the beginning and end of the row, and then follow all instructions as written for the pattern.

Option A

Option B

Reading the Charts

I get it. Charts can be scary, especially to the new knitter – I used to be a knitter that would either shy away from any pattern that had charts, or I would rewrite the chart into written instructions, simply because I had spent so much time learning the "language" of knitting (my husband is always in awe that rows and rows of instructions like "k2tog tbl, yo, k2, p2" actually make perfect sense to a knitter!).

But, hear me out on this one – charts are an essential part of colorwork. It's possible to create written instructions for colorwork (you'll find written instructions for every pattern in this book), but it can be very difficult with written instructions to visualize your colorwork. Feel free to use the written instructions in this book, but I encourage you to give the charts a try as well, you might like them!

WHAT DO MOSAIC CHARTS LOOK LIKE?

There are several different ways to chart mosaic colorwork. I prefer to create charts that look almost exactly like what you'll be knitting, while including simple instructions prior to each chart to tell you what you need to do when working the chart.

Below is the motif from the Dancing Aspens Scarf.

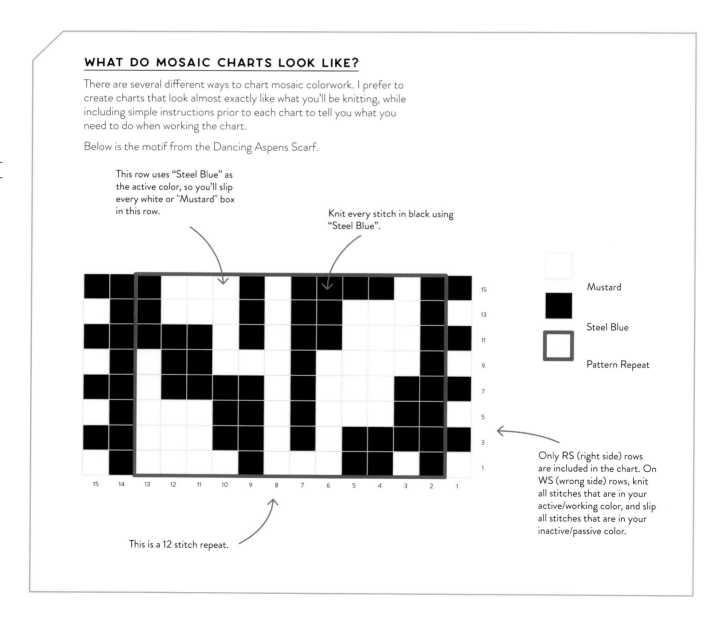

This row uses "Steel Blue" as the active color, so you'll slip every white or "Mustard" box in this row.

Knit every stitch in black using "Steel Blue".

Mustard

Steel Blue

Pattern Repeat

Only RS (right side) rows are included in the chart. On WS (wrong side) rows, knit all stitches that are in your active/working color, and slip all stitches that are in your inactive/passive color.

This is a 12 stitch repeat.

HOW TO READ THE CHARTS

First things first, you'll notice the chart is 15 stitches across and 16 rows tall (the 16th row is paired with Row 15 and isn't charted), with one selvedge (or edge) stitch before the repeat section, and two selvedge stitches after the repeat section. The edge stitches are ONLY worked at the beginning and end of each row.

The red lines on the chart are repeat lines, you will be asked to repeat what is in between the lines in order to create the charted motif.

For the example to the left, the repeat section is 12 stitches across and is repeated every 16 rows.

If you are asked to work four repeats of the motif going horizontally, you'll knit one edge stitch, work stitches 2-13 four times and then you'll work the final two edge stitches.

If you're asked to work two repeats of the motif going vertically, you'll work Rows 1-16, and then Rows 1-16 once more.

As you are knitting, you can place markers at the beginning/end of each repeat section to help you see the pattern develop.

The first thing you'll notice in the chart to the left is that only the Right Side (RS) or odd numbered rows are charted. You may see some designers include the Wrong Side (WS) rows in their charts, but I intentionally leave them out – this allows for charts with shaping elements on the RS rows, but not on the WS row (you'll see an example of this if you page ahead to the Colorplay Triangle Shawl).

Using standard colorwork conventions, you'll "read" the chart as instructions on how to work the color pattern. These charts begin at the bottom right hand corner, and work right to left, bottom to top (as is typical in most knitting charts).

The first stitch in each row indicates your "active" color. For Row 1 of the chart, the first stitch or box is white, or Mustard. Therefore you'll work across the row knitting the white stitches with Mustard, and slipping the black stitches with the yarn in back, working the repeat section as indicated in the pattern.

In other knitting styles, you would work the next row (the wrong side row) from the chart left to right... but that row isn't included in the chart! This is because the chart essentially does "double duty" – you will work the row you just finished – knitting if using garter stitch (or purling if using stockinette switch) all stitches that are in the active color and slipping all stitches purlwise with the yarn in front that are in the inactive color.

I usually tell my first-time mosaic knitters to not even look at the chart when working the WS row – just look at your knitting and knit (or purl) all the stitches in the color you are working with, and slip all other stitches purlwise with the yarn in front. It'll be okay, I promise!

After you've worked two rows in Mustard, you'll switch your yarn colors, and move onto Row 3 in the chart which begins with a black or Steel Blue stitch. The black boxes are now your "active" color – so you'll knit all the black boxes, and slip all white boxes with the yarn in the back. After the row is complete, you'll work the wrong side row by knitting (or purling) all the stitches that are in black, and slipping all stitches purlwise with the yarn in front that are in white.

INCREASES AND DECREASES IN MOTIFS

You'll find that the Colorplay Triangle Shawl uses increases on every RS row in order to achieve its triangular shape. Working increases and decreases in mosaic colorwork isn't complicated. Here is what you'll do:

Work the increase/decrease stitch on the Right Side row (usually a M1L/M1R or k2tog/ssk) in the active color.

When you arrive at the increased/decreased stitch on the Wrong Side row, you will simply knit the stitch if using garter stitch, or purl the stitch if using stockinette stitch.

A NOTE ON PATTERN DIFFICULTY

Since the focus of this book is on knitting mosaic motifs for beginners, I avoided any complex shaping, and stuck to accessories where gauge (tension) and size don't matter significantly. But, if you would like, I included one pattern with shaping that you can play around with.

Keep an eye out for the difficulty symbol at the beginning of every pattern, this will help you determine if you can binge your favorite show while knitting or if you'll need all the lights on and a quiet space to work the pattern.

STEP-BY-STEP GUIDE

In the diagrams below, you'll see several rows of garter stitch, then one repeat of Rows 1-16 of the chart from the Dancing Aspens Scarf, and the knitter is now working the second repeat of Rows 1-2.

Diagram 1: Row 1 (RS): With Mustard, knit all the white stitches.

Diagram 2: Row 1 (RS): Slip all the black stitches with the yarn held in back.

Diagram 3: Row 2 (WS): With Mustard, knit all the stitches in Mustard.

Diagram 4: Row 2 (WS): Slip all the stitches in Steel Blue with the yarn held in front.

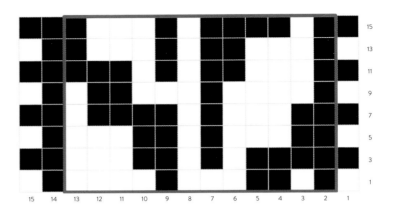

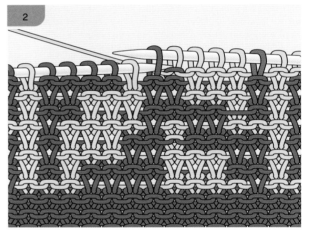

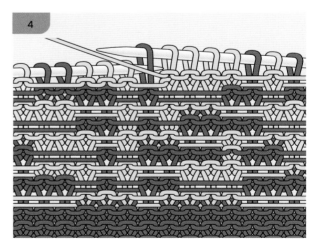

Tools and Materials

I've always loved the simplicity behind the idea of knitting – all you need are two needles and you can turn a simple string into just about anything using a bit of grit and gumption. However, sometimes certain yarns work better than others, needle size does matter, and there are some tools of the trade to make the whole process a bit easier. Here are my recommendations for tools and materials you can use to make the patterns in this book a success.

YARN

The yarn in this book ranges from 4 ply cotton to super chunky acrylic and wool blends. You can use any yarn of a similar weight and fiber content, but you might need a different quantity than the amount stated in the pattern – this is due to fiber composition and slight differences in yarn weight even within the same weight category. It's usually a good idea to grab an extra skein of each color, just in case (you can always keep the receipt or make another project with any extra).

Feel free to break the mold and choose a completely different weight yarn if you want to! At the beginning of most patterns, I include a short description of how to increase or decrease the number of repeats in the pattern in order to scale the design up or down in size. For example, it could be fun to work more repeats of the Sunday Morning Blanket in a DK or 4 ply yarn in order to create a lightweight summer blanket!

Again, if you change the weight of the yarn, the size of your pattern and yarn requirements will change – so I always recommend making a small swatch with whatever yarn you select, to check not only the gauge (tension), but to make sure you like the feel of the fabric and how the colors work together. You can use the conversion table below to help translate between UK, Australian, and US yarn weights.

All of the yarn in this book is machine washable – but I don't recommend throwing them in the dryer.

I always like to wet block my projects if the yarn is a natural fiber, either through a gentle cycle in the washing machine (if the yarn is machine washable) or a quick soak in a sink with wool-friendly soap for the more delicate yarn, and then laying them out on one of my daughter's foam play mats with a few straight pins.

If your yarn is 100% acrylic, I highly recommend steam blocking (see Techniques: Steam Blocking). You'll find if your yarn has a high percentage of acrylic, it won't block as well as yarn that is primarily natural fibers – but it will still help your yarn lay a bit more flat and even.

US	UK	AUSTRALIA	RECOMMENDED NEEDLE SIZE (METRIC)
Lace	1 ply	2 ply	1.5-2.25mm
Fingering	2 ply	3 ply	2.25-3mm
Sock	3 ply	3 ply	2.25-3.5mm
Sport	4 ply	5 ply	3.5-4.5mm
DK Light Worsted	DK	8 ply	4.5-5.5mm
Worsted	Aran	10 ply	5.5-6.5mm
Bulky	Chunky	12 ply	6.5-9mm
Super Bulky	Super Chunky	14 ply	9mm or larger

NEEDLES

For most of these projects, your gauge (tension) isn't essential. It really isn't a big deal if your shawl or blanket end up slightly larger or smaller than expected.

However, most knitters find mosaic knitting to be a bit tighter than a traditional garter or stockinette stitch (this is due to the small "floats" that occur at the back of your work when you slip stitches) – so for each pattern in this book, you'll find that I suggest you move up a needle size each time you work colorwork, and go back to a smaller size when working the rest of the pattern. This is not a hard and fast rule, there are some knitters who find their gauge is looser in colorwork, and other lucky knitters whose gauge doesn't change. Knit with the needles that work for you!

That being said, the projects in this book use a variety of needle sizes, so it might be helpful to have several needle sizes on hand when working through this book. You might need to size up or size down in order to achieve your desired gauge or fabric, and you'll find most patterns use at least two needle sizes throughout.

I love keeping a set of interchangeable circular needles in my knitting bag at all times, but all of these patterns could be worked on straight needles if that is what you prefer (although the blankets might get a bit unwieldy on straight needles!).

All of my patterns list suggested needle sizes in both UK metric and US needle sizes. The table here can also help with the conversion if you are using different needle sizes than what is listed in the pattern.

US	UK
0	2mm
1	2.25mm
1.5	2.5mm
2	2.75mm
2.5	3mm
3	3.25mm
4	3.5mm
5	3.75mm
6	4mm
7	4.5mm
8	5mm
9	5.5mm
10	6mm
10.5	6.5mm
11	8mm
13	9mm
15	10mm

OTHER SUPPLIES

You'll find that many projects in this book require additional tools – many of which you might already have, such as crochet hooks, pillow forms, pieces of cardboard to make tassels, etc. Look for this information at the beginning of each pattern where you'll find a list of everything you'll need before you begin. You'll need blocking mats, pins, a measuring tape, and a tapestry needle for every project, so I omitted them from the required tools section of each pattern.

Remember, you are free to make adjustments and customize any project to your own liking! If you don't like tassels, but love pom poms – throw some pom poms on your Berry Bramble Floor Mat! If you want to add buttons or a zipper to your Wild West Pillows so you can remove the pillow form, go right ahead. Sometimes the customization of a project is the most fun part.

Choosing Colors

Now that you're armed with everything you need to know about charts, let's jump into one of the most fun parts about starting a new project – picking out your colors!

Color selection is almost an art form when it comes to colorwork knitting, and it can be a deeply personal choice. Colors are often an expression of creativity, mood, personality, or just simply colors that you are drawn to. Use colors that you love, but don't be afraid to try a new combination – they might surprise you!

Now, not all color combinations will work equally well – and sometimes it's hard to predict whether colors will work well together without creating a swatch. I can't tell you how many colors I've tried that contrast at first glance, but when I start knitting, my colorwork becomes muddied and almost disappears – this is particularly so with yarn with speckles or gradients. On the other hand, sometimes colorways can surprise you with how well they work together!

Most of the time, using colors that contrast strongly with each other will look best. But, how can you figure this out?

Do you remember talking about hue and value in art class in school? I kind of do, so let's have a refresher!

Color wheel showing hue

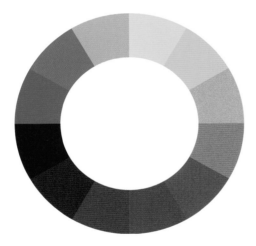

Color wheel showing value

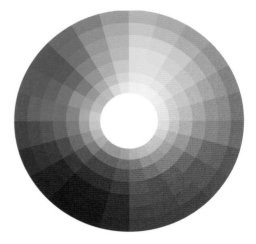

HUE

Hue is often defined as the dimension of color that we experience when we look at and describe a color – i.e. purple, red, green, yellow, etc. These are the colors that you typically see on a color wheel. Hues that are across from each other on the color wheel often contrast well with each other (orange with blue or purple are a favorite combination of mine to play with).

VALUE

But, hue isn't the most important element of color to determine if two colors will work well together. This is where value comes in. Value is the relative lightness or darkness of colors. Choosing colors that are the same value can lead to colorwork that can be hard to see, it is much easier to get bold and vibrant colorwork by choosing colors that are different values (the hue of the color could even be the same as long as the value is different – a light green and a dark green can create a gorgeous motif).

THE COLOR SHORTCUT YOU'VE BEEN WAITING FOR

Knowing this basic color theory is fun, but can often be confusing when standing in a store or looking at your stash trying to plan your next project, so I have an easy trick for you! Simply take a photo of your yarn choices and convert it to black and white. The camera app in your smartphone likely has a black and white setting. If you can tell a significant difference between the colors of yarn when you take a black and white photo, the colorways will likely work well together in mosaic colorwork.

Let's see it in action. Below are photos of some different colors of yarn – you'll notice that the yarn in the first row has significant contrast when photographed in black and white, while the second row has hardly any contrast – your colorwork will work much better in the colors of the first row than the second row.

When all else fails, simply make a swatch of the two colors you want to put together, take a few steps away from your work, and decide if the colors are working for you – sometimes the most unconventional color combinations create striking colorwork!

THE PROJECTS

From afghans, pillows, dishcloths, and works of art to keep your neck warm, each of the projects contained in this book can be starting points for your own inspiration! You'll find full written instructions and a chart for each motif – choose the method that works best for you, grab your yarn and some needles, and get started! Each motif can be easily modified into a different size by either increasing/decreasing the number of repeats (I help you out with the math to change the number of repeats at the beginning of each pattern), or by changing the weight of your yarn – the possibilities are endless!

Deja BREW COASTERS

I bet you can't make just one of these Deja Brew Coasters, when you can make an entire set in just a short afternoon, and your favorite coffee drinks will always have a safe place on your table. Grab a cup of your favorite caffeinated beverage and make one (or two or three or four!).

You Will Need

YARN

Lion Brand Wool Ease Thick & Quick (80% acrylic, 20% wool), super bulky, 170g (97m/106yds), in the following shades:

- Fisherman (099); 1 ball
- Raspberry (112); 1 ball
- Mustard (158); 1 ball
- Fig (146); 1 ball
- Lollipop (191); 1 ball

KNITTING NEEDLES

- 9mm (US 13) needles
- 10mm (US 15) needles

GAUGE (TENSION)

13 sts and 25 rows measure 15 x 14cm (6 x 5½in) over garter mosaic motif using 10mm needles and over garter stitch using 9mm needles.

Gauge is not critical for these patterns.

FINISHED SIZE

Approximately 15 x 14cm (6 x 5½in) after steam blocking

Pattern Notes

The coasters are worked flat in a small rectangle in garter stitch.

On all right side rows, slip all of the slipped stitches with yarn in back.

On all wrong side rows, slip all of the slipped stitches with yarn in front.

If you would like to change the sizing of this pattern, cast on a multiple of 10+3 sts. For example, 10x1=10. 10+3=13 cast on stitches.

Chart Notes

Each square represents a stitch. The chart begins at the lower right corner on Row 1.

Only RS (odd numbered) rows are charted and are read from right to left.

The color of the first stitch in the chart always determines the active color used for the next two rows.

For the coaster, you will work across the chart just once, so you can ignore the red repeat section lines. I've included the lines for the repeat section in case you want to work the motif on a larger project.

PATTERN

Note: The instructions below are to make the Fisherman and Raspberry sample. Simply change colors as you see fit!

SET-UP

Using 9mm needles and Raspberry, cast on 13 sts using a long tail cast on.

Row 1 (WS): K.

Rows 2 to 3: Using Fisherman, k.

Change to 10mm needles.

MOSAIC MOTIF

Follow either the written instructions or the charted instructions below.

WRITTEN INSTRUCTIONS

Row 1 (RS): With Raspberry, k1, sl1, k9, sl1, k1.

Row 2 and all WS rows: K the same sts as k in previous row, with the active color; and slip all of the same slipped sts as slipped in previous row, wyif.

Row 3: With Fisherman, k2, sl1, k7, sl1, k2.

Row 5: With Raspberry, [k1, sl1] two times, k5, [sl1, k1] two times.

Row 7: With Fisherman, k2, sl1, k1, sl1, k3, sl1, k1, sl1, k2.

Row 9: With Raspberry, [k1, sl1] 6 times, k1.

Row 11: As Row 7.

Row 13: As Row 5.

Row 15: As Row 3.

Row 17: As Row 1.

Row 19: With Fisherman, k.

CHART INSTRUCTIONS

Row 1 (RS): With Raspberry, work Row 1 of chart pattern.

Row 2 and all WS rows: K the same sts as k in previous row, with the active color; and slip all of the same slipped sts as slipped in previous row, wyif.

Continue working from the chart as set, for another 18 rows, to complete the chart.

FINISHING

Change to 9mm needles.

Rows 1 to 2: Using Raspberry, k.

Cast off all sts using a knitted cast off. Weave in ends, block as desired.

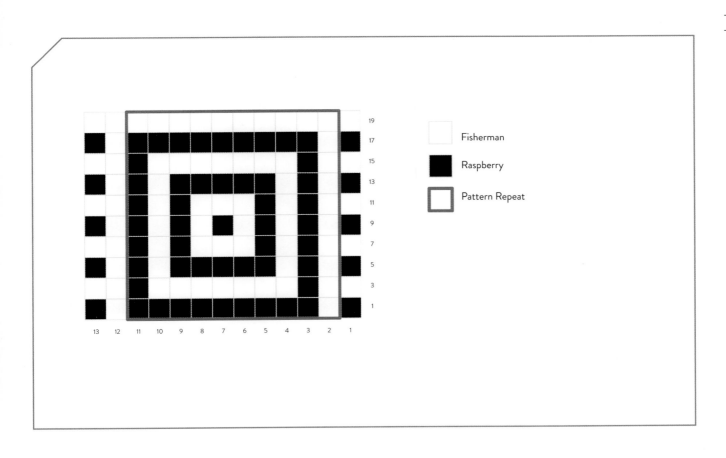

	Fisherman
	Raspberry
	Pattern Repeat

Alternative Colorway

Yarn

Lion Brand Wool Ease Thick & Quick (80% acrylic, 20% wool), super bulky, 170g (97m/106yds), in the following shades:

- Fig (146)
- Arctic Ice (648D)

Needles

Same as pattern.

Gauge (tension)

Same as pattern.

You can use any motif in this book to create whatever you would like! In this sample, I used Fig and Arctic Ice to work two vertical and horizontal repeats of the Deja Brew Coaster by repeating Stitches 2-11 and then adding in a row of garter stitch after Row 18. By increasing the number of repeats, you could make a fun and mesmerizing blanket!

Desert Rose
VANITY
TOWELS

Small desert flowers adorn this face cloth and towel duo. With an easy to memorize motif, these vanity towels are a great introduction to mosaic knitting.

These two patterns allow you to experiment with which color you use as your primary color. The face cloth uses Vintage as the primary color, while the vanity towel features Spice.

You Will Need

YARN

Lion Brand Pima Cotton (100% cotton), worsted, 100g (170m/186 yds), in the following shades:

- Vintage (099R); 2 balls
- Spice (135); 2 balls

KNITTING NEEDLES

- 4.5mm (US 7) needles
- 5mm (US 8) needles

OTHER TOOLS AND MATERIALS

- Stitch markers (optional)

GAUGE (TENSION)

21 sts and 42 rows measure 10 x 10cm (4 x 4in) over garter mosaic motif using 5mm needles.

Gauge is not critical for this pattern but may affect yarn requirements.

FINISHED SIZE
Face Cloth
19 x 18cm (7.5 x 7in) after blocking

Vanity Towel
31 x 56cm (12 x 22in) after blocking

Pattern Notes

Both the face cloth and vanity towel are worked flat in a rectangle using the same mosaic motif except the colors are reversed in the charts.

While working the motif, on all right side rows slip all of the slipped stitches with yarn in back, and on all wrong side rows slip all of the slipped stitches with yarn in front.

If you would like to change the sizing of this pattern, cast on a multiple of 12+17 sts. For example, 12x2=24. 24+17=41 cast on stitches.

Chart Notes

Each square represents a stitch. The chart begins at the lower right corner on Row 1.

Only RS (odd numbered) rows are charted and are read from right to left.

The color of the first stitch in the chart always determines the active color used for the next two rows.

DESERT ROSE FACE CLOTH

PATTERN

SET-UP

Using 4.5mm needles and Vintage, cast on 41 sts using a long tail cast on.

Set-Up Row 1 (WS): With Vintage, k to end. (41 sts)

Set-Up Rows 2 to 3: With Spice, k to end.

Set-Up Rows 4 to 5: With Vintage, k to end.

Change to 5mm needles.

MOSAIC MOTIF

If you wish to use markers for the repeats, place a marker after the first four stitches, and then every 12 sts to the final 13 stitches. Follow either the written instructions or the charted instructions below.

WRITTEN INSTRUCTIONS

Row 1 (RS): With Spice, k2, sl1, k1, *sl1, k1, sl1, k3, [sl1, k1] 3 times; rep from * twice more; k1.

Row 2 and all WS rows: K the same sts as k in previous row, with the active color; and slip all of the same slipped sts as slipped in previous row, wyif.

Row 3: With Vintage, k4, *k3, sl3, k6; rep from * twice more, k1.

Row 5: With Spice, k2, sl1, k1, *sl1, k7, [sl1, k1] 2 times; rep from * twice more, k1.

Row 7: With Vintage, k4, *k1, sl3, k1, sl3, k4; rep from * twice more, k1.

Row 9: As Row 5.

Row 11: As Row 3.

Row 13: As Row 1.

Row 15: With Vintage, k to end.

Row 17: With Spice, k2, sl1, k1, *[sl1, k1] 4 times, sl1, k3; rep from * one more time, [sl1, k1] 5 times, sl1, k2.

Row 19: With Vintage, k4, [k9, sl3] 2 times, k to end.

Row 21: With Spice, k2, sl1, k1, *k2, [sl1, k1] 2 times, sl1, k5; rep from * one more time, k2, [sl1, k1] 2 times, sl1, k3, sl1, k2.

Row 23: With Vintage, k3, sl1, *sl2, k5, sl3, k1, sl1; rep from * one more time, sl2, k5, sl3, k3.

Row 25: As Row 21.

Row 27: As Row 19.

Row 29: As Row 17.

Row 31: With Vintage, k to end.

Rows 33 to 64: As Rows 1-32.

CHART INSTRUCTIONS

Row 1 (RS): With Spice, work Row 1 of Face Cloth chart pattern, working repeat two times.

Row 2 and all WS rows: K the same sts as k in previous row, with the active color; and slip all of the same slipped sts as slipped in previous row wyif.

Continue working from the chart as set, for another 30 rows, to complete the chart.

Rows 33 to 64: As Rows 1-32.

FINISHING

Change to 4.5mm needles.

Rows 65 to 66: With Spice, k to end.

Rows 67 to 68: With Vintage, k to end.

Cast off sts using an Icelandic cast off using Vintage (see Techniques: Icelandic Cast Off) or a cast off of your choice. Weave in ends, block as desired.

FACE CLOTH

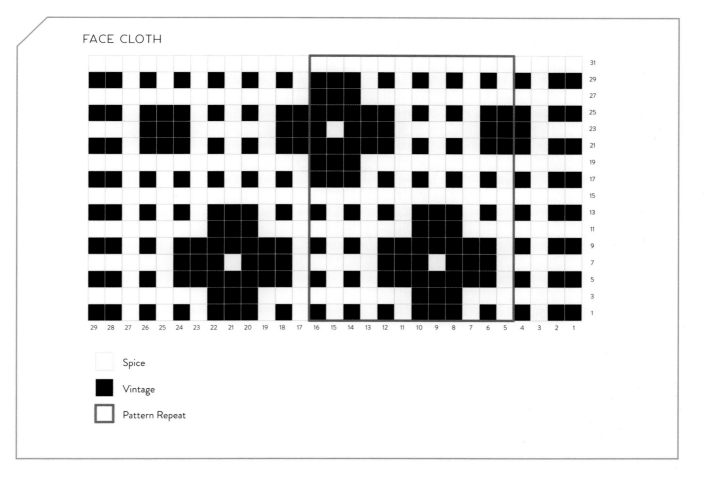

☐ Spice

■ Vintage

☐ Pattern Repeat

DESERT ROSE VANITY TOWEL

PATTERN

SET-UP

Using 4.5mm needles and Spice, cast on 65 sts using a long tail cast on.

Set-Up Row 1 (WS): With Spice, k to end. (65 sts)

Set-Up Rows 2 to 3: With Vintage, k to end.

Set-Up Rows 4 to 5: With Spice, k to end.

Change to 5mm needles.

SECTION 2: MOSAIC MOTIF

If you wish to use markers for the repeats, place a marker after the first four stitches, and then every 12 sts to the final 13 stitches. Follow either the written instructions or the charted instructions below.

WRITTEN INSTRUCTIONS

Row 1 (RS): With Vintage, k2, sl1, k1, *sl1, k1, sl1, k3, [sl1, k1] 3 times; rep from * four more times; k1.

Row 2 and all WS rows: K the same sts as k in previous row, with the active color; and slip all of the same slipped sts as slipped in previous row, wyif.

Row 3: With Spice, k4, *k3, sl3, k6; rep from * four more times, k1.

Row 5: With Vintage, k2, sl1, k1, *sl1, k7, [sl1, k1] two times; rep from * four more times, k1.

Row 7: With Spice, k4, *k1, sl3, k1, sl3, k4; rep from * four more times, k1.

Row 9: As Row 5.

Row 11: As Row 3.

Row 13: As Row 1.

Row 15: With Spice, k to end.

Row 17: With Vintage, k2, sl1, k1, *[sl1, k1] 4 times, sl1, k3; rep from * three more times, [sl1, k1] 5 times, sl1, k2.

Row 19: With Spice, k4, [k9, sl3] 4 times, k to end.

Row 21: With Vintage, k2, sl1, k1, *k2, [sl1, k1] 2 times, sl1, k5; rep from * three more times, k2, [sl1, k1] 2 times, sl1, k3, sl1, k2.

Row 23: With Spice, k3, sl1, *sl2, k5, sl3, k1, sl1; rep from * three more times, sl2, k5, sl3, k3.

Row 25: As Row 21.

Row 27: As Row 19.

Row 29: As Row 17.

Row 31: With Spice, k to end.

Rows 33 to 48: As Rows 1-16.

CHART INSTRUCTIONS

Row 1 (RS): With Vintage, work Row 1 of Vanity Towel chart pattern, working repeat four times.

Row 2 and all WS rows: K the same sts as k in previous row, with the active color; and slip all of the same slipped sts as slipped in previous row wyif.

Continue working from the chart as set, for another 30 rows, to complete the chart.

Rows 33 to 48: As Rows 1-16 of chart pattern.

SECTION 3: SINGLE SLIP STITCH

Row 1: With Vintage, k2, [sl1, k1] until 1 st remains, k1.

Row 2: K the same sts as k in previous row in Vintage; and slip all of the same slipped sts as slipped in previous row, wyif.

Rows 3 to 4: With Spice, k to end.

Rep Rows 1-4, 31 more times (or as many times as desired).

SECTION 4: MOSAIC MOTIF

Rep Section 2: Mosaic Motif.

SECTION 5: FINISHING

Change to 4.5mm needles.

With Vintage, k two rows.

With Spice, k two rows.

Cast off sts using an Icelandic cast off using Spice (see Techniques: Icelandic Cast Off) or a cast off of your choice. Weave in ends, block as desired.

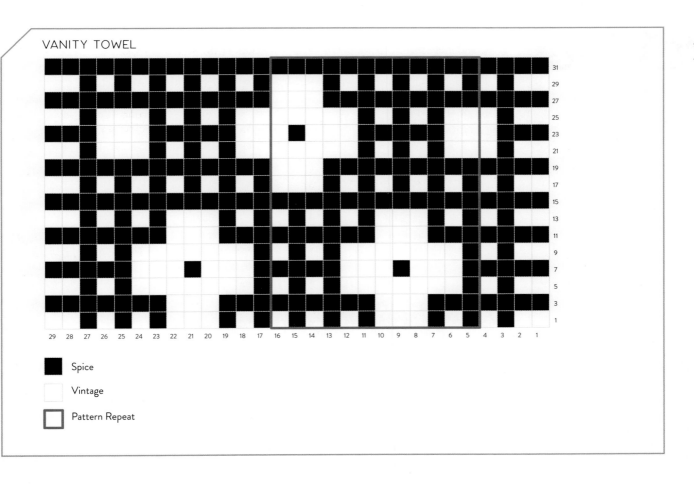

VANITY TOWEL

Spice

Vintage

Pattern Repeat

Alternative Colorway

Yarn

Lion Brand 24/7 Cotton Yarn (100% mercerized cotton), worsted, 100 g (170m/186yds), in the following shades:

- Lime (170J)
- Magenta (144L)

Needles

Same as pattern.

Gauge (tension)

Same as pattern.

After making a perfectly neutral set of vanity towels in burnt orange and cream, I wanted to make something completely different – 24/7 Cotton in Magenta and Lime make a perfect summer face cloth. For this larger version of the face towel, I cast on 65 stitches and worked the repeat section a total of four times.

Zig and Zag KITCHEN CLOTHS

Is it possible to make washing dishes and cleaning countertops fun? Probably not, but it's always fun to create a decorative dishcloth and dish towel to add a bit of flair to your kitchen. Cotton is the best fiber to use for dishcloths and towels – and it becomes more absorbent after it's been washed a few times. You can make both the dishcloth and tea towel using just two balls of Lion Brand Pima Cotton in Dragonfly, and one ball in Vintage.

You Will Need

YARN

Lion Brand Pima Cotton (100% cotton), worsted, 100g (170m/186yds), in the following shades:

• Vintage (099R); 1 ball
• Dragonfly (178Y); 2 balls

KNITTING NEEDLES

• 4.5mm (US 7) needles
• 5mm (US 8) needles

OTHER TOOLS AND MATERIALS

• Stitch markers (optional)

GAUGE (TENSION)

21 sts and 42 rows measure 10 x 10cm (4 x 4in) over garter mosaic motif using 5mm needles and over double seed stitch using 4.5mm needles.

Gauge is not critical for this pattern but may affect yarn requirements.

FINISHED SIZE

Dishcloth

19 x 19cm (7.5 x 7½in) after blocking

Dish Towel

31 x 69cm (12 x 27in) after blocking

Pattern Notes

The dishcloth and dish towel are worked flat in a rectangle using the same mosaic motif.

While working the motif, on all right side rows slip all of the slipped stitches with yarn in back, and on all wrong side rows slip all of the slipped stitches with yarn in front.

If you would like to change the sizing of this pattern, cast on a multiple of 18+5 sts. For example, 18x2=36. 36+5=41 cast on stitches.

Chart Notes

Each square represents a stitch. The chart begins at the lower right corner on Row 1.

Only RS (odd numbered) rows are charted and are read from right to left.

The color of the first stitch in the chart always determines the active color used for the next two rows.

The same chart is used for both the dishcloth and the towel.

ZIG AND ZAG DISHCLOTH

PATTERN

SET-UP

Using 4.5mm needles and Dragonfly, cast on 41 sts using a long tail cast on.

Set-Up Row 1 (WS): With Dragonfly, k to end. (41 sts)

Set-Up Rows 2 to 3: With Vintage, k to end.

Change to 5mm needles.

MOSAIC MOTIF

If you wish to use markers for the repeats, place a marker after the first two stitches, and then every 18 sts to the final three stitches.

Follow either the written instructions or the charted instructions below.

WRITTEN INSTRUCTIONS

Row 1 (RS): With Dragonfly, k2, *sl2, k1, sl1, [k3, sl1] 3 times, k1, sl1; rep from * one more time, sl1, k2.

Row 2 and all WS rows: K the same sts as k in previous row, with the active color; and slip all of the same slipped sts as slipped in previous row, wyif.

Row 3: With Vintage, k2, *k4, sl1, k3, sl1, k1, sl1, k3, sl1, k3; rep from * one more time, k3.

Row 5: With Dragonfly, k2, *k1, [sl1, k3] 4 times, sl1; rep from * one more time, k3.

Row 7: With Vintage, k2, *k2, sl1, k3, sl1, k5, sl1, k3, sl1, k1; rep from * one more time, k3.

Row 9: With Dragonfly, k2, *[k3, sl1] 4 times, k2; rep from * one more time, k3.

Row 11: With Vintage, k2, *[sl1, k3] 2 times, sl1, k1, [sl1, k3] 2 times; rep from * one more time, sl1, k2.

Row 13: With Dragonfly, k2, *k1, sl1, k3, sl1, k7, sl1, k3, sl1; rep from * one more time, k3.

Row 15: With Vintage, k2, *k2, sl1, k3, sl1, k1, sl3, k1, sl1, k3, sl1, k1; rep from * one more time, k3.

Row 17: With Dragonfly, k.

Row 19: With Vintage as Row 1.

Row 21: With Dragonfly as Row 3.

Row 23: With Vintage as Row 5.

Row 25: With Dragonfly as Row 7.

Row 27: With Vintage as Row 9.

Row 29: With Dragonfly as Row 11.

Row 31: With Vintage as Row 13.

Row 33: With Dragonfly as Row 15.

Row 35: With Vintage k.

Rows 37 to 72: As Rows 1-36.

CHART INSTRUCTIONS

Row 1 (RS): With Dragonfly, work Row 1 of chart pattern, working repeat section two times.

Row 2 and all WS rows: K the same sts as k in previous row, with the active color; and slip all of the same slipped sts as slipped in previous row wyif.

Continue working from the chart as set, for another 34 rows, to complete the chart.

Rows 37 to 72: As Rows 1-36.

FINISHING

Change to 4.5mm needles.

Rows 73 to 74: With Dragonfly, k.

Cast off sts using an Icelandic cast off and Dragonfly (see Techniques: Icelandic Cast Off) or a cast off of your choice. Weave in ends, block as desired (or just start using your dishcloth!).

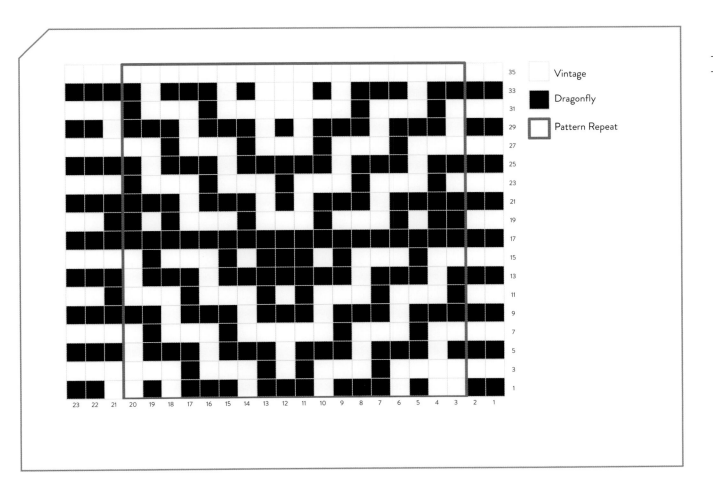

Vintage

Dragonfly

Pattern Repeat

ZIG AND ZAG TEA TOWEL

PATTERN

SET-UP

Using 4.5mm needles and Dragonfly, cast on 58 sts using a long tail cast on.

Set-Up Row (WS): [p2, k2] to 2 sts remaining, p2. (58 sts)

SECTION 1: DOUBLE SEED STITCH

Row 1 (RS): [k2, p2] to 2 sts remaining, k2.

Row 2: [p2, k2] to 2 sts remaining, p2.

Row 3: Rep Row 2.

Row 4: Rep Row 1.

Rep Rows 1-4 eight more times.

Set-Up Row 1 (RS): K28, kfb, k29. (59 sts)

Set-Up Row 2: K to end.

Change to 5mm needles.

SECTION 2: MOSAIC MOTIF

If you wish to use markers for the repeats, place a marker after the first two stitches, and then every 18 sts to the final three stitches.

Follow either the written instructions or the charted instructions below.

WRITTEN INSTRUCTIONS

Row 1 (RS): With Dragonfly, k2, *sl2, k1, sl1, [k3, sl1] 3 times, k1, sl1; rep from * two more times, sl1, k2.

Row 2 and all WS rows: K the same sts as k in previous row, with the active color; and slip all of the same slipped sts as slipped in previous row, wyif.

Row 3: With Vintage, k2, *k4, sl1, k3, sl1, k1, sl1, k3, sl1, k3; rep from * two more times, k3.

Row 5: With Dragonfly, k2, *k1, [sl1, k3] 4 times, sl1; rep from * two more times, k3.

Row 7: With Vintage, k2, *k2, sl1, k3, sl1, k5, sl1, k3, sl1, k1; rep from * two more times, k3.

Row 9: With Dragonfly, k2, *[k3, sl1] 4 times, k2; rep from * two more times, k3.

Row 11: With Vintage, k2, *[sl1, k3] 2 times, sl1, k1, [sl1, k3] 2 times; rep from * two more times, sl1, k2.

Row 13: With Dragonfly, k2, *k1, sl1, k3, sl1, k7, sl1, k3, sl1; rep from * two more times, k3.

Row 15: With Vintage, k2, *k2, sl1, k3, sl1, k1, sl3, k1, sl1, k3, sl1, k1; rep from * two more times, k3.

Row 17: With Dragonfly, k.

Row 19: With Vintage as Row 1.

Row 21: With Dragonfly as Row 3.

Row 23: With Vintage as Row 5.

Row 25: With Dragonfly as Row 7.

Row 27: With Vintage as Row 9.

Row 29: With Dragonfly as Row 11.

Row 31: With Vintage as Row 13.

Row 33: With Dragonfly as Row 15.

Row 35: With Vintage k.

Rows 37 to 72: As Rows 1-36.

CHART INSTRUCTIONS

Row 1 (RS): With Dragonfly, work Row 1 of chart pattern, working repeat section three times.

Row 2 and all WS rows: K the same sts as k in previous row, with the active color; and slip all of the same slipped sts as slipped in previous row wyif.

Continue working from the chart as set, for another 34 rows, to complete the chart.

Rows 37 to 72: As Rows 1-36.

SECTION 3: DOUBLE SEED STITCH

Change to 4.5mm needles.

Set-Up Row 1 (RS): K28, k2tog, k29. (58 sts)

Set-Up Row 2: K to end.

Rep Rows 1-4 of Section 1: Double Seed Stitch a total of 20 times (or as many times as desired).

SECTION 4: MOSAIC MOTIF

Set-Up Row 1 (RS): K28, kfb, k29. (59 sts)

Set-Up Row 2: K to end.

Change to 5mm needles.

Rep Section 2: Mosaic Motif.

SECTION 5: DOUBLE SEED STITCH

Set-Up Row 1 (RS): K28, k2tog, k29. (58 sts)

Set-Up Row 2: K to end.

Rep Rows 1-4 of Section 1: Double Seed Stitch a total of nine times.

Cast off sts using an Icelandic cast off and Dragonfly (see Techniques: Icelandic Cast Off) or a cast off of your choice. Weave in ends, block as desired (or just start using your new dish towel!).

Alternative Colorway

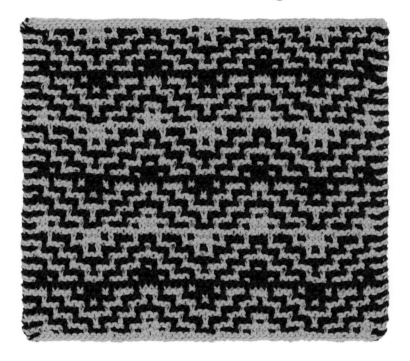

Yarn

Lion Brand 24/7 Cotton Yarn (100% mercerized cotton), worsted, 100 g (170m/186yds), in the following shades:

- Aqua (102A)
- Beets (146AM)

Needles

Same as pattern.

Gauge (tension)

Same as pattern.

I made an extra large dishcloth by casting on 59 stitches and working the repeat a total of three times instead of the original two times. This generous size and brighter colors are a great addition to my kitchen! The undulating waves of the Zig and Zag motif make the waves appear as if they are always in motion (just like my busy little kitchen – there is always something cooking or baking in my oven or a countertop to be cleaned off!).

Berry
BRAMBLE
FLOOR MAT

The mesmerizing dots within the diamonds of this motif remind me of my favorite summer fruit – berries! This cozy rug transforms any floor space with a spunky pop of yellow and comforting blues and purples. Knit up this rug in no time using super bulky yarn and an easy to memorize motif!

You Will Need

YARN

Lion Brand Wool Ease Thick & Quick (80% acrylic, 20% wool), super bulky, 170g (97m/106yds), in the following shades:

- Fisherman (099); 2 balls
- Petrol Blue (109); 1 ball
- Fig (146); 1 ball
- Mustard (158); 1 ball

KNITTING NEEDLES

- 8mm (US 11) needles
- 9mm (US 13) needles

OTHER TOOLS AND MATERIALS

- Stitch markers (optional)
- Cardboard rectangle measuring approximately 30 x 15cm (12 x 6in)
- Crochet hook (to apply fringe)

GAUGE (TENSION)

11 sts and 22 rows measure 10 x 10cm (4 x 4in) over garter mosaic motif using 9mm needles.

FINISHED SIZE

48 x 85cm (19 x 33½in) after blocking without fringe

48 x 110cm (19 x 43in) with fringe

Pattern Notes

The rug is worked flat in a rectangle.

On all right side rows, slip all of the slipped stitches with yarn in back.

On all wrong side rows, slip all of the slipped stitches with yarn in front.

For the edges, on all right side rows, the first stitch is knit through the back loop, while the last stitch is slipped with the yarn in front. On all wrong side rows, the first stitch is knit, and the last stitch is slipped with the yarn in front – this creates a clean edge. Feel free to knit the first and last stitch, or choose a different edge if you would like a different look.

If you would like to change the sizing of this pattern, cast on a multiple of 12+5 sts. For example, 12x4=48. 48+5=53 cast on stitches.

Chart Notes

Each square represents a stitch. The chart begins at the lower right corner on Row 1.

Only RS (odd numbered) rows are charted and are read from right to left.

The color of the first stitch in the chart always determines the active color used for the next two rows.

PATTERN

SET-UP

Using 8mm needles and Fisherman, cast on 53 sts using a long tail cast on.

Set-Up Row (WS): With Fisherman, k1 tbl, k to last st, sl1 wyif. (53 sts)

Change to 9mm needles.

If you wish to use markers for the repeats, place a marker after the first two stitches, and then every 14 sts to the final three stitches.

Follow either the written instructions or the charted instructions below.

WRITTEN INSTRUCTIONS

Row 1 (RS): With Petrol Blue, k1 tbl, k1, *[sl1, k1] two times, sl1, k2, [k1, sl1] two times, k1; rep from * three more times, sl1, k1, sl1 wyif.

Row 2 and all WS rows: K the same sts as k in previous row, with the active color; and slip all of the same slipped sts as slipped in previous row, wyif, to the last st, sl1 wyif.

Row 3: With Fisherman, k1 tbl, k1, *k5, sl1, k1, sl1, k4; rep from * three more times, k2, sl1 wyif.

Row 5: With Petrol Blue, k1 tbl, k1, *[k1, sl1] 2 times, k5, sl1, k1, sl1; rep from * three more times, sl1, k1, sl1 wyif.

Row 7: With Fisherman, k1 tbl, k1, *k4, [sl1, k1] 3 times; k2; rep from * three more times, k2, sl1 wyif.

Row 9: With Petrol Blue, k1 tbl, k1, *sl1, k1, sl1, k7, sl1, k1; rep from * three more times, sl1, k1, sl1 wyif.

Row 11: With Fisherman, k1 tbl, k1, *k3, [sl1, k1] 4 times, k1; rep from * three more times, k2, sl1 wyif.

Row 13: With Petrol Blue, k1 tbl, k1, * k1, sl1, k9, sl1; rep from * three more times, k2, sl1 wyif.

Row 15: With Fisherman, k1 tbl, k1 *k2, [sl1, k1] 5 times; rep from * three more times, k2, sl1 wyif.

Row 17: With Petrol Blue, k1 tbl, k to last st, sl1 wyif.

Row 19: As Row 15.

Row 21: As Row 13.

Row 23: As Row 11.

Row 25: As Row 9.

Row 27: As Row 7.

Row 29: As Row 5.

Row 31: As Row 3.

Row 33: As Row 1.

Row 35: With Fisherman, k to last st, sl1 wyif.

Rows 37 to 72: As Rows 1-36, using Fig in place of Petrol Blue.

Rows 73 to 108: As Rows 1-36, using Mustard in place of Petrol Blue.

Rows 109 to 144: As Rows 1-36, using Fig in place of Petrol Blue.

Rows 145 to 180: As Rows 1-36.

CHART INSTRUCTIONS

Row 1 (RS): With Petrol Blue, work Row 1 of chart pattern, working repeat section four times.

Row 2 and all WS rows: K the same sts as k in previous row, with the active color; and slip all of the same slipped sts as slipped in previous row, wyif, to the last st, sl1 wyif.

Continue working from the chart as set, for another 34 rows, to complete the chart.

Rows 37 to 72: As Rows 1-36, using Fig in place of Petrol Blue.

Rows 73 to 108: As Rows 1-36, using Mustard in place of Petrol Blue.

Rows 109 to 144: As Rows 1-36, using Fig in place of Petrol Blue.

Rows 145 to 180: As Rows 1-36.

FINISHING

Change to 8mm needles.

Row 181: With Fisherman, k1 tbl, k to last st, sl1 wyif.

Row 182: As Row 181.

Cast off sts using an Icelandic cast off and Fisherman (see Techniques: Icelandic Cast Off) or a cast off of your choice. Weave in ends, block as desired. Apply fringe approximately 14cm (5½in) in length along the cast on and cast off edges as desired (see Techniques: Adding Fringe).

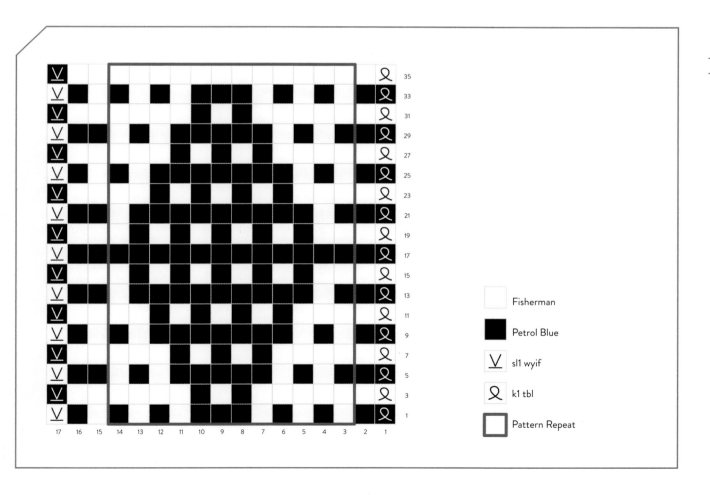

Fisherman

Petrol Blue

⋁ sl1 wyif

Ω k1 tbl

☐ Pattern Repeat

Alternative Colorway

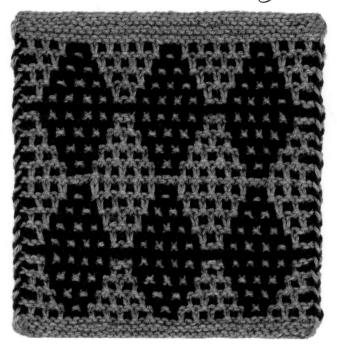

Yarn

Lion Brand Wool Ease Yarn (80% acrylic, 20% wool), worsted, 85 g (180m/197yds), in the following shades:

- Riverside (009)
- Rose Heather (140)

Needles

- 5.5mm (US 9) needles
- 6mm (US 10) needles

Gauge (tension)

19 sts and 25 rows measures 10 x 10cm (4 x 4in) over garter mosaic motif using 6mm (US 10) needles.

The Berry Bramble motif works great in many different colors. I chose to work a two-color version in Wool Ease Yarn, a machine washable worsted weight yarn. Smaller needles and lighter yarn create a more delicate version of the motif that would work great for a baby blanket – or if you choose to use cotton yarn, it would make a perfectly textured dishcloth! This pattern is easily memorizable and is a great one to practice your mosaic knitting skills.

Diamond
CRIB
BLANKET

I've always loved baby items that have unconventional colors and modern patterns – this blanket is my twist on the traditional crib sized blanket (although it can easily be adapted to make a larger afghan or a smaller car seat blanket). The bulky weight yarn knits up quickly and makes a warm blanket perfect for cool winter nights.

You Will Need

YARN
Lion Brand Hue + Me (80% acrylic, 20% wool), bulky, 125g (125m/137yds), in the following shades:

• Grapefruit (104P); 4 balls
• Sea Glass (172S); 4 balls

KNITTING NEEDLES
• 9mm (US 13) needles
• 10mm (US 15) needles

OTHER TOOLS AND MATERIALS
• Stitch markers (optional)

GAUGE (TENSION)
13 sts and 22 rows measure 10 x 10cm (4 x 4in) over garter mosaic motif using 10mm needles.

Gauge is not critical for this pattern but may affect yarn requirements.

FINISHED SIZE
84 x 118cm (33 x 46½in) after blocking

Pattern Notes

The blanket is worked flat in a rectangle.

On all right side rows, slip all of the slipped stitches with yarn in back.

On all wrong side rows, slip all of the slipped stitches with yarn in front.

For the edges, on all right side rows, the first stitch is knit through the back loop, while the last stitch is slipped with the yarn in front. On all wrong side rows, the first stitch is knit, and the last stitch is slipped with the yarn in front – this creates a clean edge. Feel free to knit the first and last stitch, or choose a different edge if you would like a different look.

If you would like to change the sizing of this pattern, cast on a multiple of 24+23 sts. For example, 24x3=72. 72+23=95 cast on stitches.

Chart Notes

Each square represents a stitch. The chart begins at the lower right corner on Row 1.

Only RS (odd numbered) rows are charted and are read from right to left.

The color of the first stitch in the chart always determines the active color used for the next two rows.

PATTERN

SET-UP

Using 9mm needles and Sea Glass, cast on 95 sts using a long tail cast on.

Set-Up Row 1 (WS): With Sea Glass, k1 tbl, k to last st, sl1 wyif. (95 sts)

Set-Up Row 2 (RS): With Grapefruit, k1 tbl, k to last st, sl1 wyif.

Set-Up Row 3 (WS): With Grapefruit, k1 tbl, k to last st, sl1 wyif.

Change to 10mm needles.

SECTION 1: SLIP STITCH COLUMNS

Row 1 (RS): With Sea Glass, k1 tbl, [k1, sl1] rep to 2 sts remaining, k1, sl1 wyif.

Rows 2 and 4: K1tbl, k the same sts as k in previous row, with the active color; and slip all of the same slipped sts as slipped in previous row, wyif, to the last st, sl1 wyif.

Row 3: With Grapefruit, k1 tbl, k1, [k1, sl1] rep to 3 sts remaining, k2, sl1 wyif.

Rows 5 to 12: Rep Rows 1-4 three more times.

Rows 13 to 14: Rep Rows 1-2 one more time.

Change to 9mm needles.

Rows 15 to 16: With Grapefruit, k1 tbl, k to last st, sl1 wyif.

Rows 17 to 18: With Sea Glass, k1 tbl, k to last st, sl1 wyif.

Change to 10mm needles.

SECTION 2: MOSAIC MOTIF

If you wish to use markers for the repeats, place a marker after the first two stitches, and then every 24 sts to the final 23 sts. Follow either the written instructions or the charted instructions below.

WRITTEN INSTRUCTIONS

Row 1: With Grapefruit, k1 tbl, k1, *sl1, k1, sl1, [k2, sl1] 2 times, k3, [sl1, k2] 2 times, [sl1, k1] 3 times; rep from * two more times, sl1, k1, sl1, [k2, sl1] 2 times, k3, [sl1, k2] 2 times, [sl1, k1] 2 times, sl1 wyif.

Row 2 and all WS rows: K1 tbl, k the same sts as k in previous row, with the active color; and slip all of the same slipped sts as slipped in previous row, wyif, to the last st, sl1 wyif.

Row 3: With Sea Glass, k1 tbl, k1, *k3, [sl1, k2] 2 times, sl3, [k2, sl1] 2 times, k6; rep from * two more times, k3, [sl1, k2] 2 times, sl3, [k2, sl1] 2 times, k4, sl1 wyif.

Row 5: With Grapefruit, k1 tbl, k1, *k1, [sl1, k2] 2 times, sl1, k5, [sl1, k2] 2 times, [sl1, k1] 2 times, sl1; rep from * two more times, k1, [sl1, k2] 2 times, sl1, k5, [sl1, k2] 3 times, sl1 wyif.

Row 7: With Sea Glass, k1 tbl, k1, *[k2, sl1] 2 times, k2, sl2, k1, sl2, [k2, sl1] 2 times, k5; rep from * two more times, [k2, sl1] 2 times, k2, sl2, k1, sl2, [k2, sl1] 2 times, k3, sl1 wyif.

Row 9: With Grapefruit, k1 tbl, k1, *[sl1, k2] 2 times, [sl1, k3] 2 times, [sl1, k2] 2 times, [sl1, k1] 2 times; rep from * two more times, [sl1, k2] 2 times, [sl1, k3] 2 times, [sl1, k2] 2 times, sl1, k1, sl1 wyif.

Row 11: With Sea Glass, k1 tbl, k1, *k1, [sl1, k2] 2 times, sl2, k3, sl2, [k2, sl1] 2 times, k4; rep from * two more times, k1, [sl1, k2] 2 times, sl2, k3, sl2, [k2, sl1] 2 times, k2, sl1 wyif.

Row 13: With Grapefruit, k1 tbl, k1, *[k2, sl1] 2 times, k3, sl1, k1, sl1, k3, [sl1, k2] 2 times, sl1, k1, sl1; rep from * two more times, [k2, sl1] 2 times, k3, sl1, k1, sl1, k3, [sl1, k2] 2 times, k1, sl1 wyif.

Row 15: With Sea Glass, k1 tbl, k1, *[sl1, k2] 2 times, sl2, k2, sl1, k2, sl2, [k2, sl1] 2 times, k3; rep from * two more times, [sl1, k2] 2 times, sl2, k2, sl1, k2, sl2, [k2, sl1] 2 times, k1, sl1 wyif.

Row 17: With Grapefruit, k1 tbl, k1, *k1, sl1, k2, sl1, [k3, sl1] 3 times, [k2, sl1] 2 times, k1; rep from * two more times, k1, sl1, k2, sl1, [k3, sl1] 3 times, k2, sl1, k2, sl1 wyif.

Row 19: With Sea Glass, k1 tbl, k1, *k2, sl1, k2, sl2, k2, sl1, k1, sl1, k2, sl2, [k2, sl1] 2 times, k1, sl1; rep from * two times, k2, sl1, k2, sl2, k2, sl1, k1, sl1, k2, sl2, k2, sl1, k3, sl1 wyif.

Row 21: With Grapefruit, k1 tbl, k1, *sl1, k2, sl1, k3, sl1, k5, sl1, k3, sl1, k2, sl1, k3; rep from * two more times, sl1, k2, sl1, k3, sl1, k5, sl1, k3, sl1, k2, sl1, k1, sl1 wyif.

Row 23: With Sea Glass, k1 tbl, k1, *k1, sl1, k2, sl2, k2, sl1, k3, sl1, k2, sl2, k2, sl1, k2, sl1, k1; rep from * two more times, k1, sl1, k2, sl2, k2, sl1, k3, sl1, k2, sl2, k2, sl1, k2, sl1 wyif.

Row 25: With Grapefruit, k1 tbl, k1, *k2, sl1, k3, sl1, k7, sl1, k3, sl1, k2, sl1, k1, sl1; rep from * two more times, k2, sl1, k3, sl1, k7, [sl1, k3] 2 times, sl1 wyif.

Row 27: With Sea Glass, k1 tbl, k1, *sl1, k2, sl2, k2, sl1, k5, sl1, k2, sl2, k2, sl1, k3; rep from * two more times, sl1, k2, sl2, k2, sl1, k5, sl1, k2, sl2, k2, sl1, k1, sl1 wyif.

Row 29: With Grapefruit, k1 tbl, k1, *k1, sl1, k3, sl1, k9, sl1, k3, sl1, k2, sl1, k1; rep from * two more times, k1, sl1, k3, sl1, k9, sl1, k3, sl1, k2, sl1 wyif.

Row 31: With Sea Glass, k1 tbl, k1, *k2, sl2, k2, sl1, k7, sl1, k2, sl2, k2, sl1, k1, sl1; rep from * two more times, k2, sl2, k2, sl1, k7, sl1, k2, sl2, k3, sl1 wyif.

Row 33: With Grapefruit, k1 tbl, k1, *sl1, k3, sl1, k11, [sl1, k3] 2 times; rep from * two more times, sl1, k3, sl1, k11, sl1, k3, sl1, k1, sl1 wyif.

Row 35: With Sea Glass, k1 tbl, k1, *k1, sl2, k2, sl1, k9, sl1, k2, sl2, k4; rep from * two more times, k1, sl2, k2, sl1, k9, sl1, k2, sl2, k2, sl1 wyif.

Row 37: With Grapefruit, k1 tbl, k1, *k3, sl1, k13, sl1, k3, sl3; rep from * two more times, k3, sl1, k13, sl1, k4, sl1 wyif.

Row 39: As Row 35.

Row 41: As Row 33.

Row 43: As Row 31.

Row 45: As Row 29.

Row 47: As Row 27.

Row 49: As Row 25.

Row 51: As Row 23.

Row 53: As Row 21.

Row 55: As Row 19.

Row 57: As Row 17.

Row 59: As Row 15.

Row 61: As Row 13.

Row 63: As Row 11.

Row 65: As Row 9

Row 67: As Row 7.

Row 69: As Row 5.

Row 71: As Row 3.

Rows 73 to 216: Rep Rows 1-72 two more times.

Row 217: As Row 1

Row 218: As Row 2

CHART INSTRUCTIONS

Row 1 (RS): With Grapefruit, work Row 1 of chart pattern, working repeat section three times.

Row 2 and all WS rows: K the same sts as k in previous row, with the active color; and slip all of the same slipped sts as slipped in previous row, wyif, to the last st, sl1 wyif.

Continue working from the chart as set, for another 70 rows, to complete the chart.

Rows 73 to 216: Rep Rows 1-72 of the chart two more times.

Rep Rows 1-2 of the chart one more time.

SECTION 3: SLIP STITCH COLUMNS AND FINISHING

Change to 9mm needles.

Set-Up Row 1 (RS): With Sea Glass, k1 tbl, k to last st, sl1 wyif.

Set-Up Row 2: With Sea Glass, k1 tbl, k to last st, sl1 wyif.

Set-Up Row 3: With Grapefruit, k1 tbl, k to last st, sl1 wyif.

Set-Up Row 4: With Grapefruit, k1 tbl, k to last st, sl1 wyif.

Change to 10mm needles.

Rep Rows 1-18 of Slip Stitch Columns from Section 1.

Cast off sts using an Icelandic cast off and Sea Glass (see Techniques: Icelandic Cast Off) or a cast off of your choice. Weave in ends, block as desired.

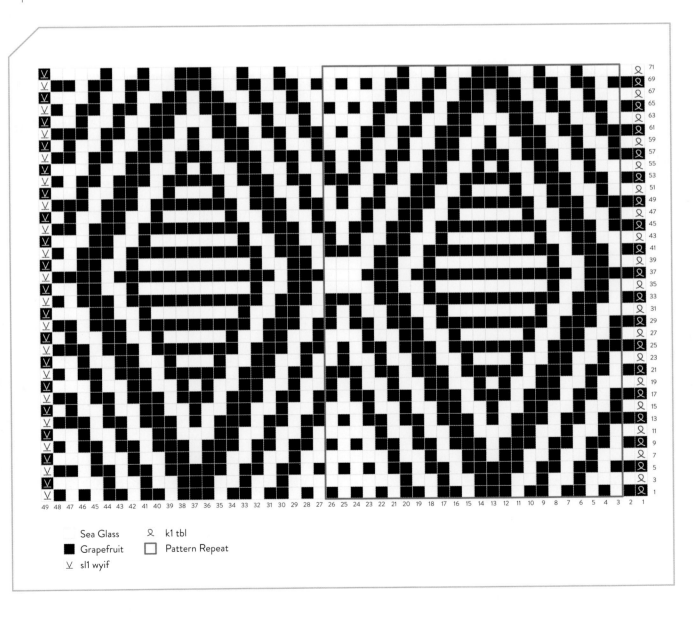

Sea Glass

■ Grapefruit

⌵ sl1 wyif

Ω k1 tbl

☐ Pattern Repeat

Alternative Colorway

Yarn

Lion Brand Feels Like Butta Yarn (100% polyester), worsted, 100g (199m/218yds), in the following shades:

- Cranberry (138)
- Golden Sunshine (159U)

Needles

- 4.5mm (US 7) needles
- 5mm (US 8) needles

Gauge (tension)

23 sts and 43 rows measures 10 x 10cm (4 x 4in) over garter mosaic motif using 5mm (US 8) needles.

Feels Like Butta is an absolutely dreamy worsted weight yarn to work with! I chose the vibrant Cranberry and Golden Sunshine colorways to make this motif come alive. If you want to make a smaller, more lightweight version of your Diamond Crib Blanket, follow the instructions as written in the pattern, but use Feels Like Butta (or another favorite worsted weight yarn) and go down to a size 4.5 or 5mm needle.

Dancing
ASPENS
SCARF

My youngest daughter was born in September in Utah, high up in the Rocky Mountains. The week following her birth, my little family went on a short hike up to see the aspens changing colors. I distinctly remember my oldest daughter exclaiming, "The leaves are dancing!" – it sure felt like they were! The aspen forest had recently turned into remarkable hues of golden leaves and the fall breeze was blowing the little golden leaves all around us. This scarf reminds me of the contrast of the vibrant gold leaves against the bluer than blue mountain sky!

You Will Need

YARN

Lion Brand Basic Stitch (100% acrylic), worsted, 100g (170m/185yd), in the following shades:

- Steel Blue (109); 2 balls
- Mustard (158); 2 balls

KNITTING NEEDLES

- 6mm (US 10) needles
- 6.5mm (US 10.5) needles

OTHER TOOLS AND MATERIALS

- Stitch markers (optional)

GAUGE (TENSION)

18 sts and 32 rows measure 10 x 10cm (4 x 4in) over garter mosaic motif using 6.5mm needles.

FINISHED SIZE

27 x 173cm (10.6 x 68in) after steam blocking

Pattern Notes

The scarf is worked flat in a rectangle.

On all right side rows, slip all of the slipped stitches with yarn in back.

On all wrong side rows, slip all of the slipped stitches with yarn in front.

If you would like to change the sizing of this pattern, cast on a multiple of 12+3 sts. For example, 12x4=48. 48+3=51 cast on stitches.

Chart Notes

Each square represents a stitch. The chart begins at the lower right corner on Row 1.

Only RS (odd numbered) rows are charted and are read from right to left.

The color of the first stitch in the chart always determines the active color used for the next two rows.

PATTERN

SET-UP

Using 6mm needles and Steel Blue, cast on 51 sts using a long tail cast on.

Set-Up Row (WS): With Steel Blue, k. (61 sts)

Change to 6.5mm needles.

If you wish to use markers for the repeats, place a marker after the first stitch, and then every 12 sts to the final two stitches.

Follow either the written instructions or the charted instructions below.

Row 1 (RS): With Mustard, k1, *sl1, k1, sl2, k3, sl1, k4; rep from * three more times, sl1, k1.

Row 2 and all WS rows: K the same sts as k in previous row, with the active color; and slip all of the same slipped sts as slipped in previous row, wyif.

Row 3: With Steel Blue, k1, *k4, sl1, k1, sl1, k2, sl3; rep from * three more times, k2.

Row 5: With Mustard, k1, *sl2, k3, sl1, k1, sl2, k3; rep from * three more times, sl1, k1.

Row 7: With Steel Blue, k1, *k2, sl3, k1, sl1, k4, sl1; rep from * three more times, k2.

Row 9: With Mustard, k1, *sl1, k4, sl1, k3, sl2, k1; rep from * three more times, sl1, k1.

Row 11: With Steel Blue, k1, *k1, sl3, k2, sl1, k1, sl1, k3; rep from * three more times, k2.

Row 13: With Mustard, k1, *sl1, k3, sl2, k1, sl1, k3, sl1; rep from * three more times, sl1, k1.

Row 15: With Steel Blue, k1, *k1, sl1, k4, sl1, k1, sl3, k1; rep from * three more times, k2.

Rep Rows 1-16 34 more times, or as many times as necessary to reach desired length.

CHART INSTRUCTIONS

Row 1 (RS): With Mustard, work Row 1 of chart pattern, working repeat section four times.

Row 2 and all WS rows: K the same sts as k in previous row, with the active color; and slip all of the same slipped sts as slipped in previous row, wyif, to the last st.

Continue working from the chart as set, for another 14 rows, to complete the chart.

Rep Rows 1-16 34 more times, or as many times as necessary to reach desired length.

FINISHING

Change to 6mm needles.

Set-Up Row 1 (RS): With Steel Blue, k.

Set-Up Row 2 (WS): As Set-Up Row 1.

Cast off sts using an Icelandic cast off and Steel Blue (see Techniques: Icelandic Cast Off) or a cast off of your choice.

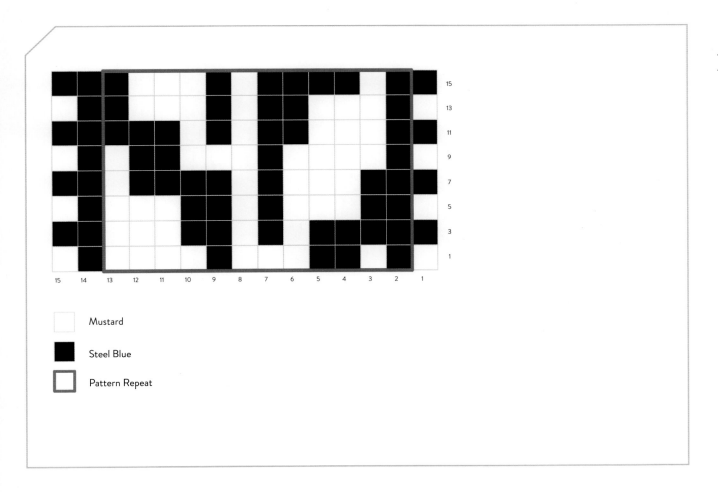

Mustard

Steel Blue

Pattern Repeat

Alternative Colorway

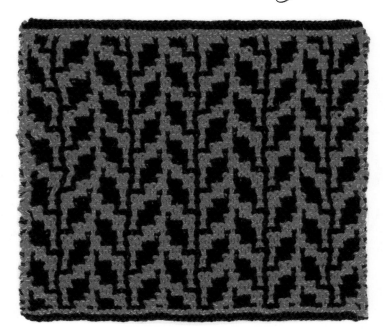

Yarn

Lion Brand Basic Stitch (100% acrylic), worsted, 100g (170m/185yds), in the following shades:

- Purple (147B); 2 balls
- Atomic Pink (305AA); 2 balls

Needles

Same as pattern.

Gauge (tension)

Same as pattern.

I've seen reflective yarn used in hats before, but never in a scarf, so I had to give it a try! Atomic Pink and Purple in Basic Stitch create an almost shocking color combination that creates a perfect, unique, and sneakily safe scarf for anyone who spends time outside in the dark during the winter. I'll be making one for my daughter who waits for the bus every morning outside our house!

Comfy
COZY
MUG COZIES

Four quick motifs make the perfect set of Mug Cozies! These simple motifs are a perfect introduction to mosaic knitting, and will keep your hot drinks hot, and your cold drinks cold! Plus, you can slip them over a small center pull ball of yarn to keep the pesky ball from unraveling on you!

You Will Need

YARN

Lion Brand BonBons (100% acrylic), DK light worsted, 80g (26m/28yds), in the following collection:

• Crayon (680); 1 set of 8 colors

KNITTING NEEDLES

• 4mm (US 6) needles
• 4.5mm (US 7) needles

GAUGE (TENSION)

21 sts and 14 rows measures approximately 10 x 5cm (4 x 2in) over stockinette mosaic motif using 4.5mm needles (due to the difference in the motifs, gauge may differ slightly between each cozy).

FINISHED SIZE

Approximately 20 x 10cm (8 x 4in) after steam blocking prior to seaming

Pattern Notes

The cozies are worked flat in a small rectangle with ribbing at the beginning and end, and a stockinette stitch mosaic motif.

Each cozy is worked in two colors, labeled as Color 1 and Color 2.

Comfy Cozy 1 used: Red and Light Orange

Comfy Cozy 2 used: Purple and Lime Green

Comfy Cozy 3 used: Green and Hot Pink

Comfy Cozy 4 used: Blue and Bright Orange

While working the mosaic motif, on all right side rows, slip all of the slipped stitches with yarn in back.

While working the mosaic motif, on all wrong side rows, slip all of the slipped stitches with yarn in front.

Chart Notes

Each square represents a stitch. The chart begins at the lower right corner on Row 1.

Only RS (odd numbered) rows are charted and are read from right to left.

The color of the first stitch in the chart always determines the active color used for the next two rows.

COMFY COZY 1

PATTERN

SET-UP

Using 4mm needles and Red, cast on 42 sts using a long tail cast on.

Set-Up Row (WS): With Red, k3, [p2, k2] until 3 sts remain, p3.

Rows 1 to 4: As Set-Up Row.

Row 5 (RS): With Light Orange, k.

Row 6: With Light Orange, p.

Change to 4.5mm needles.

MOSAIC MOTIF

If you wish to use markers for the repeats, place a marker after the first stitch, and then every 10 stitches to the last stitch.

Follow either the written instructions or the charted instructions below.

WRITTEN INSTRUCTIONS

Row 1 (RS): With Red, k1,*sl1, k9; rep from * three more times, k1.

Row 2 and all WS rows: P the same sts as k in previous row, with the active color; and slip all of the same slipped sts as slipped in previous row, wyif.

Row 3: With Light Orange, k1,*k1 [sl1, k3] 2 times, sl1; rep from * three more times, k1.

Row 5: With Red, k1,*sl1, k3, sl1, k1, sl1, k3; rep from * three more times, k1.

Row 7: With Light Orange, k1,*k5, sl1, k4; rep from * three more times, k1.

Row 9: As Row 1.

Row 11: As Row 7.

Row 13: As Row 5.

Row 15: As Row 3.

Row 17: As Row 1.

CHART INSTRUCTIONS

If desired, place a marker after the first stitch and then every 10 sts until the last stitch.

Row 1 (RS): With Red, work Row 1 of chart pattern working repeat section four times.

Row 2 and all WS rows: P the same sts as k in previous row, with the active color; and slip all of the same slipped sts as slipped in previous row, wyif.

Continue working from the chart as set, for another 16 rows, to complete the chart.

FINISHING

Change to 4mm needles.

Row 1 (RS): With Light Orange, k.

Row 2 (WS): With Light Orange, p.

Break Light Orange.

Row 3 (RS): With Red, k.

Row 4 (RS): With Red, k3, [p2, k2] until 3 sts remain, p3.

Rows 5 to 8: As Row 4.

With Red, cast off all sts using a knitted cast off in pattern. Weave in ends, block as desired. With the wrong sides facing each other, join the two shorter sides together using a mattress stitch (see Techniques: Mattress Stitch).

COMFY COZY 2

PATTERN

SET-UP

As Comfy Cozy 1 Set-Up, using Purple in place of Red and Lime Green in place of Light Orange.

MOSAIC MOTIF

If you wish to use markers for the repeats, place a marker after the first stitch, and then every 10 stitches to the last stitch.

Follow either the written instructions or the charted instructions below.

Row 1 (RS): With Purple, k1,*sl2, k7, sl1; rep from * three more times, k1.

Row 2 and all WS rows: P the same sts as k in previous row, with the active color; and slip all of the same slipped sts as slipped in previous row, wyif.

Row 3: With Lime Green, k1,*k2, sl1, k5, sl1, k1; rep from * three more times, k1.

Row 5: With Purple, k1,*[k3, sl1] 2 times, k2; rep from * three more times, k1.

Row 7: With Lime Green, k1,*k4, sl1, k1, sl1, k3; rep from * three more times, k1.

Row 9: With Purple, k1, *k5, sl1, k4; rep from * three more times, k1.

Row 11: As Row 7.

Row 13: As Row 5.

Row 15: As Row 3.

Row 17: As Row 1.

If desired, place a marker after the first stitch and then every 10 sts until the last stitch.

Row 1 (RS): With Purple, work Row 1 of chart pattern working repeat section four times.

Row 2 and all WS rows: P the same sts as k in previous row, with the active color; and slip all of the same slipped sts as slipped in previous row, wyif.

Continue working from the chart as set, for another 16 rows, to complete the chart.

FINISHING

As Comfy Cozy 1 Finishing instructions, using Purple in place of Red and Lime Green in place of Light Orange.

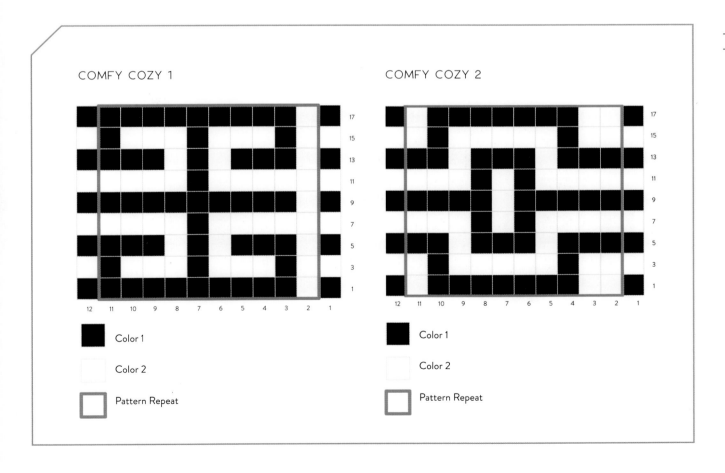

COMFY COZY 1

COMFY COZY 2

Color 1

Color 2

Pattern Repeat

COMFY COZY 3

PATTERN

SET-UP

As Comfy Cozy 1 Set-Up, using Green in place of Red and Hot Pink in place of Light Orange.

MOSAIC MOTIF

If you wish to use markers for the repeats, place a marker after the first stitch, and then every 2 stitches to the last stitch.

Follow either the written instructions or the charted instructions below.

WRITTEN INSTRUCTIONS

Row 1 (RS): With Green, k1, [sl1, k1] until 1 st remains, k1.

Row 2 and all WS rows: P the same sts as k in previous row, with the active color; and slip all of the same slipped sts as slipped in previous row, wyif.

Row 3: With Hot Pink, k.

Row 5: With Green, k1, [k1, sl1] until 1 st remains, k1.

Row 7: As Row 2.

Rows 9 to 16: As Rows 1-8.

Rows 17 to 18: As Rows 1-2.

CHART INSTRUCTIONS

Row 1 (RS): With Green, work Row 1 of chart pattern working repeat to last stitch.

Row 2 and all WS rows: P the same sts as k in previous row, with the active color; and slip all of the same slipped sts as slipped in previous row, wyif.

Continue working from the chart as set for another six rows, to complete the chart. Rep Rows 1-8 one more time, then rep Rows 1-2 one more time.

FINISHING

As Comfy Cozy 1 Finishing instructions, using Green in place of Red and Hot Pink in place of Light Orange.

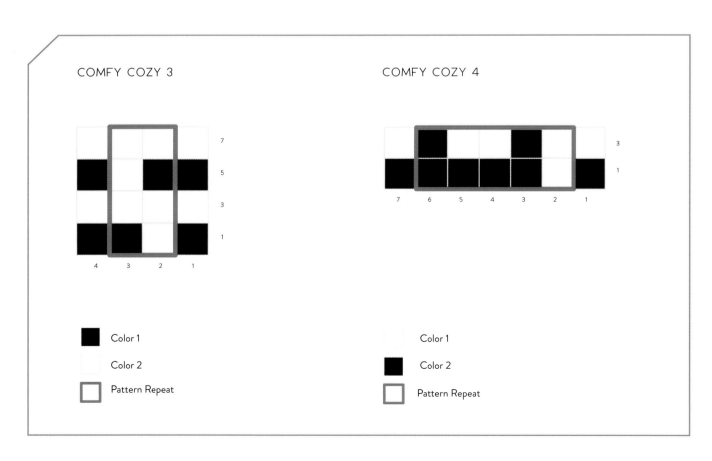

COMFY COZY 4

PATTERN

SET-UP

As Comfy Cozy 1 Set-Up, using Blue in place of Red and Bright Orange in place of Light Orange.

MOSAIC MOTIF

If you wish to use markers for the repeats, place a marker after the first stitch, and then every 5 stitches to the last stitch.

Follow either the written instructions or the charted instructions below.

WRITTEN INSTRUCTIONS

Row 1 (RS): With Blue, k1, [sl1, k4] until 1 st remains, k1.

Row 2 and all WS rows: P the same sts as k in previous row, with the active color; and slip all of the same slipped sts as slipped in previous row, wyif.

Row 3: With Bright Orange, k1, [k1, sl1, k2, sl1] until 1 st remains, k1.

Rows 5 to 16: As Rows 1-4.

Rows 17 to 18: As Rows 1-2.

CHART INSTRUCTIONS

If desired, place a marker after the first stitch and then every 5 sts until the last stitch.

Row 1 (RS): With Blue, work Row 1 of chart pattern working repeat section to last stitch.

Row 2 and all WS rows: P the same sts as k in previous row, with the active color; and slip all of the same slipped sts as slipped in previous row, wyif.

Continue working from the chart as set, for another two rows, to complete the chart. Rep Rows 1-4 three more times, then rep Rows 1-2 one more time.

FINISHING

As Comfy Cozy 1 Finishing instructions, using Blue in place of Red and Bright Orange in place of Light Orange.

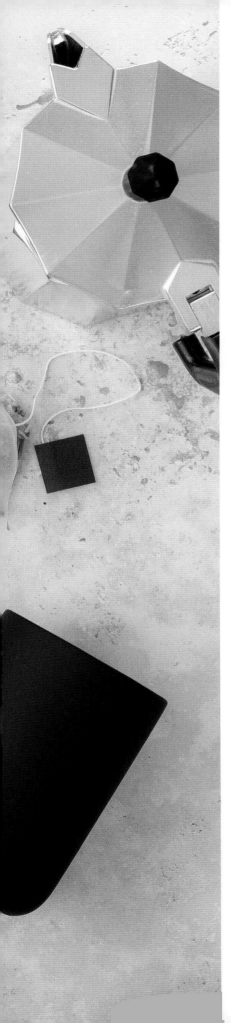

Alternative Colorway

Yarn

Lion Brand Wool Ease Thick & Quick (80% acrylic, 20% wool), super bulky, 170g (97m/106yds), in the following shade:

- Pumpkin (133A)

Lion Brand Re-Spun Thick & Quick Yarn (100% recycled polyester); super bulky, 340g (204m/223yds), in the following shade:

- Faded Denim (106BD)

Needles

- 9mm (US 13) needles
- 10mm (US 15) needles

Gauge (tension)

9 sts and 15 rows measures 10 x 10cm (4 x 4in) over mosaic motif using 10mm (US 15) needles.

I love pairing a vibrant orange like Pumpkin with a blue gray to help mellow out the bright color – using grays is a great way to make bright colors "pop". For this sample, I paired together all of the Comfy Cozy motifs on super bulky yarn just to see what they might look like together. Have fun and pair together different motifs to make something completely your own!

Tundra
TAMER
COWL

After moving back to Minnesota in the middle of winter after over 15 years away (most of which were spent deep in the heart of Texas), I quickly remembered how fashion often gets thrown out the door to function when the arctic winds start to blow! I designed this super chunky cowl with fresh pops of color to make the most frigid mornings feel a bit warmer.

If you don't need such a warm cowl, feel free to swap in a lighter weight yarn and smaller needles (you might need to add a couple of repeats to reach your desired size).

You Will Need

YARN

Lion Brand Wool Ease Thick & Quick (80% acrylic, 20% wool), super bulky, 170g (97m/106yds), in the following shades:

· Pumpkin (133A); 1 ball
· Bluegrass (550F); 1 ball
· Lollipop (191K); 1 ball

KNITTING NEEDLES

· 9mm (US 13) needles
· 10mm (US 15) needles

OTHER TOOLS AND MATERIALS

· Stitch markers (optional)

GAUGE (TENSION)

9.5 sts and 16.5 rows measure 10 x 10cm (4 x 4in) over stockinette mosaic motif using 10mm needles and over stockinette stitch using 9mm needles.

Gauge is not critical for this pattern, the fabric is very stretchy by nature, but may affect yarn requirements.

FINISHED SIZE

Approximately 40cm (15½in) deep and 71cm (28in) circumference after steam blocking

Pattern Notes

The cowl is worked flat, starting with the ribbed edge, then the mosaic motif worked in stockinette stitch, and ending with another ribbed edge. The piece is then seamed together using a mattress stitch.

On all right side rows, slip all of the slipped stitches with yarn in back.

On all wrong side rows, slip all of the slipped stitches with yarn in front.

If you would like to change the sizing of this pattern, cast on a multiple of 16+2 sts. For example, 16x4=64. 64+2=66.

When you reach the final ribbing section, increase/decrease the necessary number of stitches to return to cast on stitch count (66 sts as given in the pattern).

As you change colors throughout the pattern, you can either break the yarn, or carry the yarn along the right hand side of the work.

Chart Notes

Each square represents a stitch. The chart begins at the lower right corner on Row 1.

Only RS (odd numbered) rows are charted and are read from right to left.

The color of the first stitch in the chart always determines the active color used for the next two rows.

PATTERN

SECTION 1: RIBBING

Using 9mm needles and Bluegrass, cast on 66 sts using a long tail cast on.

Row 1 (WS): K3, [p2, k2] until 3 sts remain, p3. (66 sts)

Rows 2 to 5: As Row 1.

Change to 10mm needles.

SECTION 2: MOSAIC MOTIF

If you wish to use markers for the repeats, place a marker after the first stitch, and then every 16 sts to the final stitch.

Follow either the written instructions or the charted instructions below.

WRITTEN INSTRUCTIONS

Row 1 (RS): With Bluegrass, k.

Row 2 and all WS rows: P the same sts as k in previous row, with the active color; and slip all of the same slipped sts as slipped in previous row, wyif.

Row 3: With Pumpkin, k1, *k4, sl2, k5, sl2, k3; rep from * three more times, k1.

Row 5: With Bluegrass, k1; *k3, sl1, k2, sl1, k3, [sl1, k2] 2 times; rep from * three more times, k1.

Row 7: With Pumpkin, k1, *k2, sl1, k1, sl2, [k1, sl1] 2 times, k1, sl2, k1, sl1, k1; rep from * three more times, k1.

Row 9: With Bluegrass, k1; *sl2, k1, sl1, k2, sl1, k3, sl1, k2, sl1, k1, sl1; rep from 8 three more times, k1.

Row 11: With Pumpkin, k1; *k2, sl1, k1, sl2, k5, sl2, k1, sl1, k1; rep from * three more times, k1.

Row 13: With Bluegrass, k1; *k3, sl1, k9, sl1, k2; rep from * three more times, k1.

Row 15: With Pumpkin, k.

Row 17: With Bluegrass, k.

Rows 19 to 36: As Rows 1-18, but use Lollipop in place of Bluegrass, and use Bluegrass in place of Pumpkin.

Rows 37 to 54: As Rows 1-18, but use Pumpkin in place of Bluegrass, and use Lollipop in place of Pumpkin.

CHART INSTRUCTIONS

Row 1 (RS): With Bluegrass, work Row 1 of chart pattern, working repeat section four times.

Row 2 and all WS rows: P the same sts as k in previous row, with the active color; and slip all of the same slipped sts as slipped in previous row, wyif.

Continue working from the chart as set, for another 16 rows, to complete the chart.

Rows 19 to 36: As Rows 1-18, but use Lollipop in place of Bluegrass, and use Bluegrass in place of Pumpkin.

Rows 37 to 54: As Rows 1-18, but use Pumpkin in place of Bluegrass, and use Lollipop in place of Pumpkin.

SECTION 3: RIBBING

Change to 9mm needles and Pumpkin.

Row 1 (RS): K3, [p2, k2] until 3 sts remain, p3. (66 sts)

Rows 2 to 4: As Row 2.

Cast off all sts using Pumpkin. Weave in ends, block as desired.

FINISHING

With the wrong sides facing each other, join the two shorter sides together using a mattress stitch (see Techniques: Mattress Stitch).

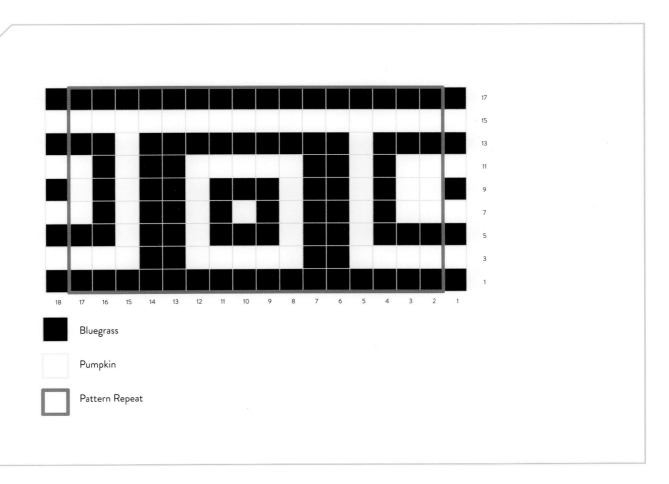

■ Bluegrass

□ Pumpkin

▢ Pattern Repeat

Alternative Colorway

Yarn

Lion Brand Hometown Yarn (100% acrylic), super bulky, 142g (74m/81 yds), in the following shades:

- Phoenix Azalea (208M)
- San Diego Navy (111L)
- Oklahoma City Green (172D)

Needles

Same as pattern.

Gauge (tension)

Same as pattern.

Just for fun, I decided to choose three jewel tone shades of Hometown Yarn and work the Tundra Tamer motif in garter stitch instead of stockinette stitch. This creates a squishier more textured version than the original cowl – it would make a wonderfully thick blanket, or fun scarf if you repeated the motif vertically a few times!

Wild
WEST
PILLOWS

The characteristically bold patterns and high contrast colors of the American Southwest hold a special place in my heart and adorn most of the corners of my house. These generously sized pillows look great on any sofa, and if you look closely, you'll see the mosaic motifs are actually the same – the only difference is that one is more bold than the other. The transformation is astonishing!

FINISHED SIZE

The pillow forms are intentionally larger than the pillow cover to make a full and fluffy pillow.

Bold Wild West Pillow

Approximately 48 x 56cm (19 x 22in) after steam blocking and prior to inserting pillow form

Tri-Color Wild West Pillow

Approximately 48 x 48cm (19 x 19in) after blocking and prior to inserting pillow form

You Will Need

YARN

For the Bold Wild West Pillow

Lion Brand Hue + Me (80% acrylic, 20% wool), bulky, 125g (125m/137yds), in the following shades:

- Werewolf (152AB); 1 ball
- Salt (098AS); 2 balls

For the Tri-Color Wild West Pillow

Lion Brand Hue + Me (80% acrylic, 20% wool), bulky, 125g (125m/137yds), in the following shades:

- Werewolf (152AB); 2 balls
- Salt (098AS); 1 ball
- Love Song (140U); 1 ball

KNITTING NEEDLES

For the Bold Wild West Pillow

- 5.5mm (US 9) needles
- 6mm (US 10) needles

For the Tri-Color Wild West Pillow

- 6mm (US 10) needles
- 6.5mm (US 10.5) needles

OTHER TOOLS AND MATERIALS

- Two 56 x 56cm (22 x 22in) pillow forms
- Stitch markers (optional)

GAUGE (TENSION)

Gauge is not critical for this pattern, the fabric is very stretchy by nature, but may affect yarn requirements.

For the Bold Wild West Pillow

12 sts and 23 rows measure 10 x 10cm (4 x 4in) over mosaic motif using 6mm needles and over stockinette stitch using 5.5mm needles.

For the Tri-Color Wild West Pillow

13 sts and 20 rows measure 10 x 10cm (4 x 4in) over mosaic motif using 6.5mm needles and over stockinette stitch using 6mm needles.

Pattern Notes

The pillows are worked in two pieces, the front piece is worked in a mosaic motif, while the back is plain stockinette. The pieces are then seamed together using a mattress stitch.

On all right side rows, slip all of the slipped stitches with yarn in back.

On all wrong side rows, slip all of the slipped stitches with yarn in front.

If you would like to change the sizing of the Tri-Color Wild West pattern, cast on a multiple of 12+13. For example, 12x4=48. 48+13=61 cast on stitches.

If you would like to change the sizing of the Bold Wild West pattern, cast on a multiple of 20+19 sts. For example, 20x2=40. 40+19=59 cast on stitches.

As you change colors throughout the patterns, you can either break the yarn, or carry the yarn along the right hand side of the work.

Chart Notes

Each square represents a stitch. The chart begins at the lower right corner on Row 1.

Only RS (odd numbered) rows are charted and are read from right to left.

The color of the first stitch in the chart always determines the active color used for the next two rows.

TRI-COLOR WILD WEST PILLOW

PATTERN: SIDE 1

Using 6mm needles and Salt, cast on 61 sts using a long tail cast on.

Set-Up Row 1 (WS): With Salt, p all sts. (61 sts)

SECTION 1: STRIPES

Row 1 (RS): With Salt, k all sts.

Row 2: With Salt, p all sts.

Row 3: With Love Song, k all sts.

Row 4: With Love Song, p all sts.

Row 5: With Werewolf, k all sts.

Row 6: With Werewolf, p all sts.

Rows 7 to 8: Rep Rows 3-4.

Rows 9 to 10: Rep Rows 1-2.

Change to 6.5mm needles.

SECTION 2: MOSAIC MOTIF

If you wish to use markers for the repeats, place a marker after the first stitch, and then every 12 sts. Follow either the written instructions or the charted instructions below.

WRITTEN INSTRUCTIONS

Row 1 (RS): With Werewolf, k1, *k1, sl1, k2, sl1, k1, [sl1, k2] 2 times; rep from * four more times.

Row 2 and all WS rows: P the same sts as k in previous row, with the active color; and slip all of the same slipped sts as slipped in previous row, wyif.

Row 3: With Salt, k1, *[k2, sl1] 4 times, rep from * three more times, [k2, sl1] 3 times, k3.

Row 5: With Werewolf, k1, *sl1, k2, sl1, k3, sl1, k2, sl1, k1; rep from * four more times.

Row 7: With Salt, k1, *sl1, k2, sl1, k1, sl1, k2, sl1, k2; rep from * four more times.

Row 9: With Werewolf, as Row 3.

Row 11: With Salt, as Row 5.

Row 13: With Love Song, as Row 7.

Row 15: With Salt, as Row 3.

Row 17: With Love Song, as Row 5.

Row 19: As Row 15.

Row 21: As Row 13.

Row 23: As Row 11.

Row 25: As Row 9.

Row 27: As Row 7.

Row 29: As Row 5.

Row 31: As Row 3.

Row 33: As Row 1.

CHART INSTRUCTIONS

Row 1 (RS): With Werewolf, work Row 1 of chart pattern, working repeat section four times.

Row 2 and all WS rows: P the same sts as k in previous row, with the active color; and slip all of the same slipped sts as slipped in previous row, wyif.

Continue working from the chart as set, for another 32 rows, to complete the chart.

NEXT STEPS

Rep Sections 1-2 one more time.

Rep Section 1 one more time.

FINISHING

Cast off all sts using Salt. Weave in ends, block as desired.

PATTERN: SIDE 2

STOCKINETTE STITCH

Using 6mm needles and Werewolf, cast on 61 sts using a long tail cast on.

Set-Up Row 1 (WS): With Werewolf, p all sts. (61 sts)

Work 98 rows in stockinette stitch (k all RS rows and p all WS rows).

Cast off all sts. Weave in ends, block as desired.

FINISHING

With the wrong sides facing each other, join the two sides together using a Mattress Stitch (see Techniques: mattress stitch). After three sides have been joined together, insert the pillow form, and join the final edges together.

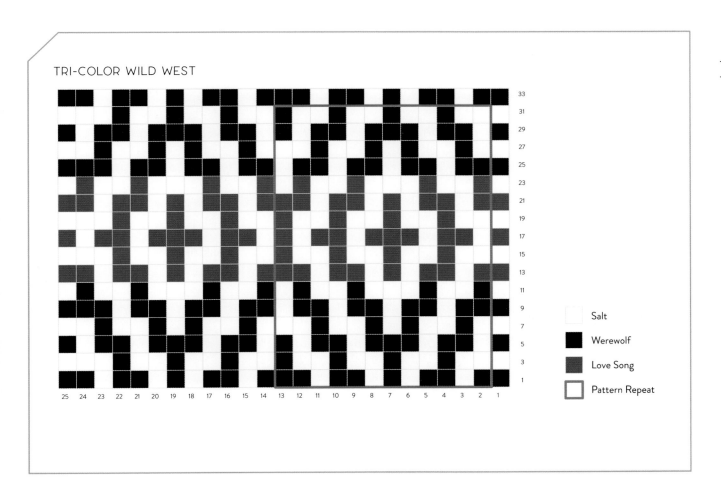

TRI-COLOR WILD WEST

Salt

Werewolf

Love Song

Pattern Repeat

BOLD WILD WEST PILLOW

PATTERN: SIDE 1

Using 5.5mm needles and Salt, cast on 59 sts using a long tail cast on.

Set-Up Row 1 (WS): With Salt, p all sts. (59 sts)

If you wish to use markers for the repeats, place a marker after the first stitch, and then every 20 sts to the final 19 sts.

Follow either the written instructions or the charted instructions below.

WRITTEN INSTRUCTIONS

Row 1 (RS): With Werewolf, k1, *k2, sl2, k3, sl1, k1, sl1, k3, sl2, k5; rep from * one more time, k2, sl2, k3, sl1, k1, sl1, k3, sl2, k3.

Row 2 and all WS rows: P the same sts as k in previous row, with the active color; and slip all of the same slipped sts as slipped in previous row, wyif.

Row 3: With Salt, k1, *k4, sl2, k2, sl1, k2, sl2, k4, sl3; rep from * one more time, k4, sl2, k2, sl1, k2, sl2, k5.

Row 5: With Werewolf, k1, *sl3, k3, [sl1, k3] 2 times, sl3, k3; rep from * one more time, sl3, k3, [sl1, k3] 2 times, sl3, k1.

Row 7: With Salt, k1, *k3, sl2, k2, sl3, k2, sl2, k4, sl1, k1; rep from * one more time, k3, sl2, k2, sl3, k2, sl2, k4.

Row 9: With Werewolf, k1, *sl2, k3, sl1, k5, sl1, k3, sl3, k1, sl1; rep from * one more time, sl2, k3, sl1, k5, sl1, k3, sl2, k1.

Row 11: With Salt, k1, *[k2, sl2] 2 times, k1, sl2, k2, sl2, k3, sl1, k1; rep from * one more time, [k2, sl2] 2 times, k1, sl2, k2, sl2, k3.

Row 13: With Werewolf, k1, *[sl1, k3] 4 times, sl2, k1, sl1; rep from * one more time, [sl1, k3] 4 times, sl1, k1.

Row 15: With Salt, k1, *k1, sl2, k2, sl2, k3, sl2, k2, sl2, k4; rep from * one more time, k1, sl2, k2, sl2, k3, sl2, k2, sl2, k2.

Row 17: With Werewolf, k1, *k3, sl1, k3, sl3, k3, sl1, k3, sl3; rep from * one more time, k3, sl1, k3, sl3, k3, sl1, k4.

Row 19: With Salt, k1, *sl2, k2, sl2, k5, sl2, k2, sl2, k3; rep from * one more time, sl2, k2, sl2, k5, sl2, k2, sl2, k1.

Row 21: With Werewolf, k1, *k2, sl1, k3, sl2, k1, sl2, [k3, sl1] 2 times, k1; rep from * one more time, k2, sl1, k3, sl2, k1, sl2, k3, sl1, k3.

Row 23: With Salt, k1, *sl1, k2, sl2, k3, sl1, k3, sl2, k2, sl2, k1, sl1; rep from * one more time; sl1, k2, sl2, k3, sl1, k3, sl2, k2, sl1, k1.

Row 25: With Werewolf, k1, *k1, sl1, k3, sl3, k1, sl3, k3, sl1, k4; rep from * one more time, k1, sl1, k3, sl3, k1, sl3, k3, sl1, k2.

Row 27: With Salt, k1, *k2, sl2, k4, sl1, k4, sl2, k2, sl3; rep from * one more time; k2, sl2, k4, sl1, k4, sl2, k3.

Row 29: With Werewolf, k1, *sl1, [k3, sl3] 2 times, k3, sl1, k3; rep from * one more time, sl1, [k3, sl3] 2 times, k3, sl1, k1.

Row 31: With Salt, k1, *k1, sl2, k4, sl3, k4, sl2, k2, sl1, k1; rep from * one more time, k1, sl2, k4, sl3, k4, sl2, k2.

Row 33: With Werewolf, k1, *k3, sl2, k7, sl2, k3, sl1, k1, sl1; rep from * one more time, k3, sl2, k7, sl2, k4.

Row 35: As Row 31.

Row 37: As Row 29.

Row 39: As Row 27.

Row 41: As Row 25.

Row 43: As Row 23.

Row 45: As Row 21.

Row 47: As Row 19.

Row 49: As Row 17.

Row 51: As Row 15.

Row 53: As Row 13.

Row 55: As Row 11.

Row 57: As Row 9.

Row 59: As Row 7.

Row 61: As Row 5.

Row 63: As Row 3.

Rows 65 to 98: Rep Rows 1-34.

CHART INSTRUCTIONS

Row 1 (RS): With Werewolf, work Row 1 of chart pattern, working repeat section twice.

Row 2 and all WS rows: P the same sts as k in previous row, with the active color; and slip all of the same slipped sts as slipped in previous row, wyif.

Continue working from the chart as set, for another 32 rows, to complete the chart.

Rows 65 to 98: Rep Rows 1-34.

FINISHING

Cast off all sts using Salt. Weave in ends, block as desired.

PATTERN: SIDE 2

STOCKINETTE STITCH

Using 6mm needles and Salt, cast on 59 sts using a long tail cast on.

Set-Up Row 1 (WS): With Salt, p all sts. (59 sts)

Work 98 rows in stockinette stitch (k all RS rows and p all WS rows).

Cast off all sts. Weave in ends, block as desired.

FINISHING

With the wrong sides facing each other, join the two sides together using a Mattress Stitch (see Techniques: mattress stitch). After three sides have been joined together, insert the pillow form, and join the final edges together.

BOLD WILD WEST

39 38 37 36 35 34 33 32 31 30 29 28 27 26 25 24 23 22 21 20 19 18 17 16 15 14 13 12 11 10 9 8 7 6 5 4 3 2 1

1 3 5 7 9 11 13 15 17 19 21 23 25 27 29 31 33 35 37 39 41 43 45 47 49 51 53 55 57 59 61 63

☐ Salt

■ Werewolf

☐ Pattern Repeat

Alternative Colorway

Yarn

Lion Brand Re-Spun Thick & Quick Yarn (100% recycled polyester), super bulky, 340g (204m/223yds), in the following shades:

- Faded Denim (106BD)
- Night Sky (110AT)
- Cinnamon Stick (133AS)

Needles

Same as pattern.

Gauge (tension)

Same as pattern

Moody grays and cinnamon show just how different a pattern can look by swapping out colors. These pillows would be a perfect addition to your fall decor (or cast on extra repeats and make an afghan!). Just for fun, I removed the horizontal stripes and worked two repeats of the Tri-Color Wild West motif by working Rows 1-32 of the mosaic motif section multiple times – let your imagination create something uniquely you.

Colorplay
TRIANGLE
SHAWL

Let your imagination roam free on this shawl! This tasseled wrap combines a classic mosaic motif with two balls of yarn with long color changes – every shawl made with this mesmerizing pattern will be completely one of a kind, as the color combinations throughout change as the colors shift in the yarn. The color shifts create unpredictable and unique color combinations each time.

You Will Need

YARN

Lion Brand Mandala Yarn (100% acrylic), DK light worsted, 150g (540m/590yds), in the following shade:

· Thunderbird (207AG); 2 balls

KNITTING NEEDLES

· 5mm (US 8) needles
· 5.5mm (US 9) needles

OTHER TOOLS AND MATERIALS

· Stitch markers

GAUGE (TENSION)

20 sts and 30 rows measure 10 x 10cm (4 x 4in) over garter mosaic motif using 5.5mm needles.

Gauge is not critical for this pattern but may affect yarn requirements.

FINISHED SIZE

162 x 64cm (64 x 25in) after steam blocking

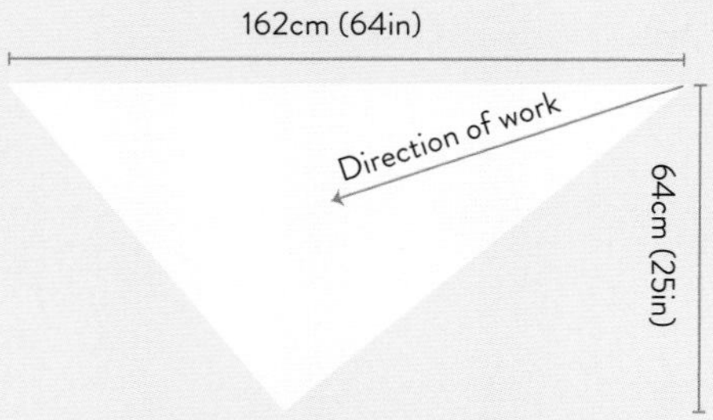

162cm (64in)

Direction of work

64cm (25in)

Pattern Notes

The shawl is worked flat starting at one corner of the triangle and then increasing by one stitch every right side row to create a large triangular shawl that can be worn in a multitude of ways.

This shawl is created by using two balls of the same color. In order to avoid confusion, I refer to the yarn as Ball 1 and Ball 2 (I found it easiest to label each ball of yarn with a tag, in case I lost my place in the pattern as the colors changed).

On all right side rows, when working the mosaic motif, knit all of the stitches in the active color, and slip all of the slipped stitches with yarn in back.

On all wrong side rows, when working the mosaic motif, purl all of the stitches in the active color, and slip all of the slipped stitches with yarn in front.

If you would like to change the sizing of this pattern, work Rows 1-64 of the motif and then repeat Rows 33-64 (increasing the number of repeats by one each time) as many times as you would like until you've reached the desired size.

Chart Notes

Each square represents a stitch. The chart begins at the lower right corner on Row 1.

Only RS (odd numbered) rows are charted and are read from right to left.

The color of the first stitch in the chart always determines the active color used for the next two rows.

PATTERN

SET-UP

Optional: If you want to create a tassel on each corner of the shawl that roughly corresponds to the colors in that part of the shawl, before casting on, reserve yarn for the first tassel by using the colors that are at the beginning of each ball of yarn. After you cast off, you'll then use the yarn from the cast off colors to create the tassels for the other two corners.

Using 5mm needles and Ball 2, cast on 5 sts using a long tail cast on.

Set-Up Rows 1, 5, 9, 13 (WS): With Ball 2, k.

Set-Up Row 2 (RS): With Ball 1, k3, m1r, k2. (6 sts)

Set-Up Rows 3, 7, 11: With Ball 1, k.

Set-Up Row 4: With Ball 2, k4, m1r, k2. (7 sts)

Set-Up Row 6: With Ball 1, k5, m1r, k2. (8 sts)

Set-Up Row 8: With Ball 2, k5, m1r, k3. (9 sts)

Set-Up Row 10: With Ball 1, k5, m1r, k4. (10 sts)

Set-Up Row 12: With Ball 2, k5, pm, m1r, pm, k5. (11 sts)

Change to 5.5mm needles.

MOSAIC MOTIF

If you wish to use markers for the repeats, keep the markers that were placed in Set-Up Row 12 and place an additional marker after stitch 6. While working Row 33, you can add a new stitch marker at the end of every 16 st repeat as the shawl grows in size.

Follow either the written instructions or the charted instructions below.

WRITTEN INSTRUCTIONS

Note: Rows 33-64 contain the pattern repeat section; this section starts with a "*" and ends with a ";". The first time you work Rows 33-64 you will only work the repeat section once, so the instructions state to "work from * once". Each time you repeat Rows 33-64, you'll increase the number of times you work the repeat section by one.

Row 1 (RS): With Ball 1, k5, sm, k1, m1r, sm, k5. (12 sts)

Row 2 and all WS rows: K5, sm, p the sts that were k in previous row, making sure to p the st created from the m1r, with the active color, and slip all of the same slipped sts as slipped in the previous row, wyif, to final marker, sm, k5.

Row 3: With Ball 2, k5, sm, k2, m1r, sm, k5. (13 sts)

Row 5: With Ball 1, k5, sm, k1, sl1, k1, m1r, sm, k5. (14 sts)

Row 7: With Ball 2, k5, sm, k2, sl1, k1, m1r, sm, k5. (15 sts)

Row 9: With Ball 1, k5, sm, [k1, sl1] 2 times, k1, m1r, sm, k5. (16 sts)

Row 11: With Ball 2, k5, sm, k4, sl1, k1, m1r, sm, k5. (17 sts)

Row 13: With Ball 1, k5, sm, k1, sl1, k3, sl1, k1, m1r, sm, k5. (18 sts)

Row 15: With Ball 2, k5, sm, k2, sl1, k3, sl1, k1, m1r, sm, k5. (19 sts)

Row 17: With Ball 1, k5, sm, k1, sl1, k3, sl1, k3, m1r, sm, k5. (20 sts)

Row 19: With Ball 2, k5, sm, k4, sl1, k3, sl1, k1, m1r, sm, k5. (21 sts)

Row 21: With Ball 1, k5, sm, [k1, sl1] 2 times, k3, sl1, k3, m1r, sm, k5. (22 sts)

Row 23: With Ball 2, k5, sm, k2, sl1, k3, sl1, k5, m1r, sm, k5. (23 sts)

Row 25: With Ball 1, k5, sm, k1, [sl1, k3] 3 times, m1r, sm, k5. (24 sts)

Row 27: With Ball 2, k5, sm, k4, sl1, k3, sl1, k1, sl1, k3, m1r, sm, k5. (25 sts)

Row 29: With Ball 1, k5, sm, [sl1, k1] 2 times, [k3, sl1] 2 times, k3, m1r, sm, k5. (26 sts)

Row 31: With Ball 2, k5, sm, k to marker, m1r, sm, k5. (27 sts)

Row 33: With Ball 1, k5, sm, k1, *sl1, k1, [sl1, k3] 3 times, sl1, k1; work from * once, m1r, sm, k5. (28 sts)

Row 35: With Ball 2, k5, sm, k1, *[k3, sl1] 2 times, k1, sl1, k3, sl1, k2; work from * once, k1, m1r, sm, k5. (29 sts)

Row 37: With Ball 1, k5, sm, k1, *[sl1, k3] 4 times; work from * once, sl1, k1, m1r, sm, k5. (30 sts)

Row 39: With Ball 2, k5, sm, k1, *k1, sl1, k3, sl1, k5, sl1, k3, sl1; work from * once, k1, sl1, k1, m1r, sm, k5. (31 sts)

Row 41: With Ball 1, k5, sm, k1, *sl1, k1, sl1, [k3, sl1] 3 times, k1; work from * once, [sl1, k1] 2 times, m1r, sm, k5. (32 sts)

Row 43: With Ball 2, k5, sm, k1, *[k3, sl1] 2 times, k1, sl1, k3, sl1, k2; work from * once, k3, sl1, k1, m1r, sm, k5. (33 sts)

Row 45: With Ball 1, k5, sm, k1, *[sl1, k3] 4 times; work from * once, sl1, k3, sl1, k1, m1r, sm, k5. (34 sts)

Row 47: With Ball 2, k5, sm, k1, *k1, sl1, k3, sl1, k5, sl1, k3, sl1 ; work from * once, k1, sl1, k3, sl1, k1, m1r, sm, k5. (35 sts)

Row 49: With Ball 1, k5, sm, k1, *[sl1, k3] 4 times; work from * once, [sl1, k3] 2 times, m1r, sm, k5. (36 sts)

Row 51: With Ball 2, k5, sm, k1, *[k3, sl1] 2 times, k1, sl1, k3, sl1, k2; work from * once, [k3, sl1] 2 times, k1, m1r, sm, k5. (37 sts)

Row 53: With Ball 1, k5, sm, k1, *sl1, k1, sl1, [k3, sl1] 3 times, k1; work from * once, sl1, k1, [sl1, k3] 2 times, m1r, sm, k5. (38 sts)

Row 55: With Ball 2, k5, sm, k1, *k1, sl1, k3, sl1, k5, sl1, k3, sl1; work from * once, k1, sl1, k3, sl1, k5, m1r, sm, k5. (39 sts)

Row 57: With Ball 1, k5, sm, k1, *[sl1, k3] 4 times; work from * once, [sl1, k3] 3 times, m1r, sm, k5. (40 sts)

Row 59: With Ball 2, k5, sm, k1, *[k3, sl1] 2 times, k1, sl1, k3, sl1, k2; work from * once, k3, sl1, k3, sl1, k1, sl1, k3, m1r, sm, k5. (41 sts)

Row 61: With Ball 1, k5, sm, k1, *sl1, k1, [sl1, k3] 3 times, sl1, k1; work from * once, sl1, k1, [sl1, k3] 3 times, m1r, sm, k5. (42 sts)

Row 63: With Ball 2, k5, sm, k to final marker, m1r, sm, k5. (43 sts)

Rep Rows 33-64, but work the repeat section (between the "*" and ";") one more time than in the previous repeat. (59 sts) Continue to Rep Rows 33-64 as many times as desired. The sample worked Rows 33-64 a total of 10 times. (187 sts)

CHART INSTRUCTIONS

Row 1 (RS): With Ball 1, k to m, sm, work Row 1 of chart pattern, sm, k5. (12 sts)

Row 2 and all WS rows: K5, sm, p the sts that were k in previous row, making sure to p the st created from the m1r, with the active color, and slip all of the same slipped sts as slipped in the previous row, wyif to final marker, sm, k5.

Continue working in garter stitch to the first marker, then from the chart as set and continuing in garter stitch after the second marker for another 62 rows, to complete the chart. (43 sts)

Rep Rows 33-64, but work the repeat section one more time than in previous repeat. (59 sts)

Continue to Rep Rows 33-64 as many times as desired. The sample worked Rows 33-64 a total of 10 times. (187 sts)

Remove markers once complete with this section.

FINISHING

Change to 5mm needles.

Set-Up Row 1: With Ball 1, k to 5 sts remaining, m1r, k5. (188 sts)

Set-Up Row 2: With Ball 1, k.

Set-Up Row 3: With Ball 2, k to 5 sts remaining, m1r, k5. (189 sts)

Set-Up Row 4: With Ball 2, k.

Rep Set-Up Rows 1-4 one more time, then work Set-Up Rows 1-2 one more time. (192 sts)

Cast off sts using an Icelandic cast off and Ball 1 (see Techniques: Icelandic Cast Off) or a cast off of your choice. Weave in ends, steam block as desired. Using the colors from the cast off edge, and the yarn reserved from the cast on, create three tassels and affix to each corner of the shawl (see Techniques: Creating Tassels).

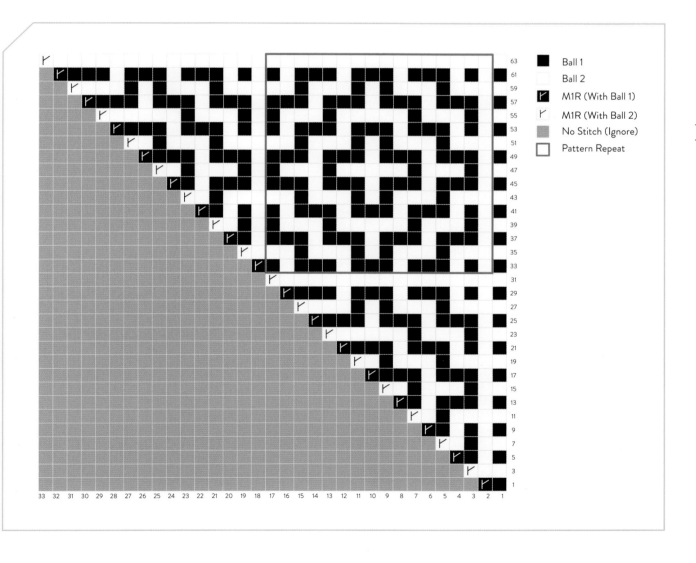

■	Ball 1
□	Ball 2
⊬	M1R (With Ball 1)
Ⱶ	M1R (With Ball 2)
▨	No Stitch (Ignore)
☐	Pattern Repeat

Alternative Colorway

Yarn

Lion Brand Mandala Yarn (100% acrylic), DK light worsted, 150g (540m/590yds), in the following shade:

- Hades (244D)

Needles

Same as pattern.

Gauge (tension)

Same as pattern.

Do you have a favorite color? Do you use it when you knit? Jewel tones are my absolute favorite colors! I worked up this sample using Hades in Mandala.

The exciting part about using yarn with long color shifts is that you have no idea what the final product will look like – this sample is an excellent example of how you can use contrast to your advantage when selecting colors – you can see how the colors blend together due to their low contrast and then the motif pops out at you just a few rows later as the colors shift.

Tic Tac Toe
WALL
HANGING

Whenever I play tic tac toe with my daughter, she always wants to be the Xs. Sometimes she likes to play this simple game by herself... and she always wins because every box contains an X! This mesmerizing tapestry is inspired by her winning game, and proves that macramé and crochet aren't the only crafts that can create beautiful wall art! The two layers of fringe create dimension and are perfect for using up yarn scraps that you might have laying around.

You Will Need

YARN

Lion Brand Wool Ease Thick & Quick (80% acrylic, 20% wool), super bulky, 170g (97m/106yds), in the following shades:

- Fisherman (099); 2 balls
- Black (153); 1 ball
- Mustard (158); 1 ball
- Bluegrass (550F); 1 ball

KNITTING NEEDLES

- 9mm (US 13) needles
- 10mm (US 15) needles

OTHER TOOLS AND MATERIALS

- Crochet hook (to apply fringe)
- Cardboard rectangle measuring approximately 30 x 23cm (12 x 9in)
- 1cm (⅜in) wooden dowel approximately 65cm (25½in) long

GAUGE (TENSION)

10.5 sts and 22 rows measure 10 x 10cm (4 x 4in) over garter mosaic motif using 10mm needles and over seed stitch using 9mm needles.

Gauge is not critical for this pattern.

FINISHED SIZE

Approximately 46 x 70cm (18 x 27½in) after steam blocking without fringe.

Approximately 46 x 89cm (18 x 35in) with fringe

Pattern Notes

The wall hanging is worked flat from the top down. The dowel is sewn onto the tapestry and fringe is added after the tapestry is bound off.

While working the motif, on all right side rows, slip all of the slipped stitches with yarn in back.

On all wrong side rows, slip all of the slipped stitches with yarn in front.

If you would like to change the sizing of this pattern, cast on a multiple of 14+5 sts. For example, 14x3=42. 42+5=47 cast on stitches.

Chart Notes

Each square represents a stitch. The chart begins at the lower right corner on Row 1.

Only RS (odd numbered) rows are charted and are read from right to left.

The color of the first stitch in the chart always determines the active color used for the next two rows.

PATTERN

SECTION 1: SEED STITCH

Using 9mm needles and Fisherman, cast on 47 sts using a long tail cast on.

The following Seed Stitch Row will be worked throughout the tapestry:

Seed Stitch Row: K2, [p1,k2] until 3 sts remain, p1, k2. (47 sts)

Set-Up Row (WS): Using Fisherman, work Seed Stitch Row.

Rows 1 to 4: Using Fisherman, work Seed Stitch Row.

Rows 5 to 6: Using Mustard, k.

Rows 7 to 18: Using Mustard, work Seed Stitch Row.

Rows 19 to 20: Using Fisherman, k.

Rows 21 to 30: Using Fisherman, work Seed Stitch Row.

Change to 10mm needles.

SECTION 2: MOSAIC MOTIF

If you wish to use markers for the repeats, place a marker after the first two stitches, and then every 14 stitches to the final three stitches.

Follow either the written instructions or the charted instructions below. The motif contains several rows where five stitches are slipped consecutively – make sure you keep the float loose to prevent the piece from puckering.

WRITTEN INSTRUCTIONS

Row 1 (RS): With Black, k2; *sl1, k4, sl5, k4; rep from * two more times, sl1, k2.

Row 2 and all WS rows: K the same sts as k in previous row, with the active color; and slip all of the same slipped sts as slipped in previous row, wyif.

Row 3: With Fisherman, k2, *k1, sl1, k2, sl1, k5, sl1, k2, sl1; rep from * two more times, k3.

Row 5: With Black, k2, *sl1, k2, sl1, k2, sl3, k2, sl1, k2; rep from * two more times, sl1, k2.

Row 7: With Fisherman, k2, *k2, sl1, k2, sl1, k3, sl1, k2, sl1, k1; rep from * two more times, k3.

Row 9: With Black, k2, *sl2, [k2, sl1] 4 times; rep from * two more times, sl1, k2.

Row 11: With Fisherman, k2, *k3, sl1, k2, sl1, k1, sl1, k2, sl1, k2; rep from * two more times, k3.

Row 13: With Black, k2, *sl3, k4, sl1, k4, sl2; rep from * two more times, sl1, k2.

Row 15: With Fisherman, k.

Row 17: As Row 13.

Row 19: As Row 11.

Row 21: As Row 9.

Row 23: As Row 7.

Row 25: As Row 5.

Row 27: As Row 3.

Row 29: As Row 1.

Row 31: As Row 15.

Rep Rows 1-32 two more times.

CHART INSTRUCTIONS

Row 1 (RS): With Black, work Row 1 of chart pattern.

Row 2 and all WS rows: K the same sts as k in previous row, with the active color; and slip all of the same slipped sts as slipped in previous row, wyif.

Continue working from the chart as set, for another 30 rows, to complete the chart.

Rep Rows 1-32 two more times.

SECTION 3: SEED STITCH

Change to 9mm needles.

Seed Stitch Row: K2, [p1,k2] until 3 sts remain, p1, k2. (47 sts)

Rows 1 to 2: Using Fisherman, k.

Rows 3 to 6: Using Fisherman, work Seed Stitch Row.

Rows 7 to 12: Using Bluegrass, rep Rows 1-6.

Rows 13 to 18: Using Fisherman, rep Rows 1-6.

Rows 19 to 24: Using Fisherman, rep Rows 1-6. The garter "bumps" created in Row 20 of this section will be used to attach the upper layer of fringe.

FINISHING

Cast off all sts using a knitted cast off. Weave in ends, block as desired.

Using Fisherman and a tapestry needle, sew the top of the tapestry onto the wooden dowel. Affix an additional piece of yarn as long as desired to either end of the dowel so that the piece can be hung.

Create fringe approximately 21cm (8½in) long (see Techniques: Adding Fringe).

Bottom Layer: Apply 47 pieces of fringe in black along the cast off edge.

Top Layer: Apply fringe to the garter stitch row created from Row 20 of Section 3 in the following pattern: 5 Fisherman, 3 Mustard, 10 Fisherman, 11 Mustard, 10 Fisherman, 3 Mustard, 5 Fisherman.

Trim fringe so both layers of fringe create a point, and the two layers of fringe are clearly visible. Fringe can be steamed to help it lay flat.

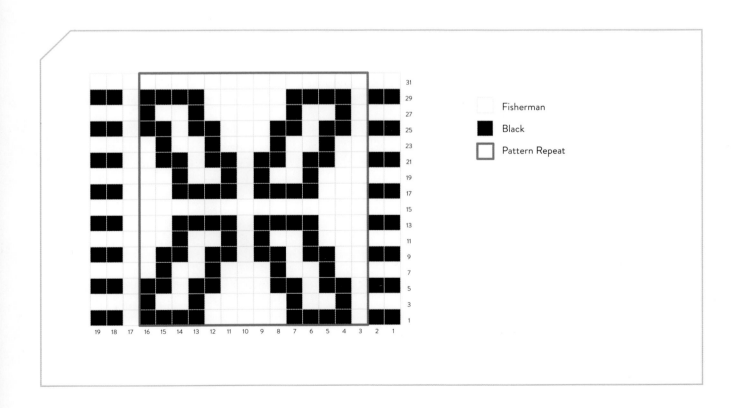

Alternative Colorway

Yarn

Lion Brand Wool Ease Thick & Quick (80% acrylic, 20% wool), super bulky, 170g (9m/106yds), in the following shades:

- Campfire (621D)
- Arctic Ice (548D)

Needles

Same as pattern.

Gauge (tension)

Same as pattern.

Absolutely striking is the only way I can describe Wool Ease Thick & Quick in Campfire and Arctic Ice. I turned the original color scheme on its head by using the deep red as the primary color, and used a pale color in place of the original black. A mustard-yellow seed stitch accent would work great with this color combination!

Saguaro
SUNSET
AFGHAN

Saguaros are solitary cacti reaching up to the sky amongst the scrub brush and tumbleweeds, whose open arms invite you to touch them, to give them a hug (even though you know it's a bad idea!). My Saguaro Sunset Afghan invokes hot desert afternoons where the temperature quickly falls as evening arrives – the long color changes imitate beautiful sunsets that you can only find in the high desert. It's hard to set this blanket down because every row you knit you get to slowly see the full motif magically emerge.

You Will Need

YARN

Lion Brand Mandala Ombre (100% acrylic), worsted, 150g (315m/344yds), in the following shade:

· Serene (207BA); 3 balls

Lion Brand Wool Ease (80% acrylic, 20% wool), worsted, 85g (180m/197yds) in the following shade:

· Rainforest (078A); 5 balls

KNITTING NEEDLES

· 5.5mm (US 9) needles
· 6mm (US 10) needles

OTHER TOOLS AND MATERIALS

· Stitch markers (optional)

GAUGE (TENSION)

19 sts and 25 rows measure 10 x 10cm (4 x 4in) over garter mosaic motif using 6mm needles.

Gauge is not critical for this pattern.

FINISHED SIZE

91 x 127cm (36 x 50in) after steam blocking

Pattern Notes

The blanket is worked flat in a rectangle in garter stitch.

On all right side rows, slip all of the slipped stitches with yarn in back.

On all wrong side rows, slip all of the slipped stitches with yarn in front.

If you would like to change the sizing of this pattern, cast on a multiple of 52+19 sts. For example, 52x3=156. 156+19=175 cast on stitches.

Chart Notes

Each square represents a stitch. The chart begins at the lower right corner on Row 1.

Only RS (odd numbered) rows are charted and are read from right to left.

The color of the first stitch in the chart always determines the active color used for the next two rows.

PATTERN

SET-UP

Using 5.5mm needles and Serene, cast on 175 sts using a long tail cast on.

Set-Up Row (WS): Using Serene, k all sts.

Rows 1 to 2: Using Rainforest, k all sts.

Rows 3 to 4: Using Serene, k all sts.

Change to 6mm needles.

MOSAIC MOTIF

If you wish to use markers for the repeats, place a marker after the first ten stitches, and then every 52 stitches to the final nine stitches.

Follow either the written instructions or the charted instructions below.

WRITTEN INSTRUCTIONS

Row 1 (RS): With Rainforest, k all sts.

Row 2 and all WS rows: K the same sts as k in previous row, with the active color; and slip all of the same slipped sts as slipped in previous row, wyif.

Row 3: With Serene, k10, [sl1, k1] until 9 sts remain, k9.

Row 5: As Row 1.

Row 7: With Serene, k10, *k8, sl2, [k1, sl1] 18 times, sl1, k5; rep from * two more times, k9.

Row 9: With Rainforest, k10, *[sl2, k1] 2 times, sl2, k39, sl1, k1, sl2, k1; rep from * two more times, k9.

Row 11: With Serene, k10, *k14, [sl1, k1] 2 times, sl1, k7, sl2, [k1, sl1] 8 times, sl1, k7; rep from * two more times, k9.

Row 13: With Rainforest, k10, *[sl2, k1] 4 times, sl2, k5, [sl2, k1] 2 times, sl1, k19, sl3, k1, sl2, k1; rep from * two more times, k9.

Row 15: With Serene, k10, *k14, sl2, k1, sl2, k12, sl2, [k1, sl1] 4 times, sl1, k10; rep from * two more times, k9.

Row 17: With Rainforest, k10, *[sl2, k1] 3 times, sl1, k9, [sl2, k1] 3 times, sl3, k11, sl3, [k1, sl2] 2 times, k1; rep from * two more times, k9.

Row 19: With Serene, k10, *k10, [sl1, k1] 4 times, sl1, k15, sl2, k1, sl2, k13; rep from * two more times, k9.

Row 21: With Rainforest, k10, *[sl2, k1] 2 times, sl2, k11, [sl2, k1] 4 times, sl3, k9, [sl2, k1] 3 times; rep from * two more times, k9.

Row 23: With Serene, k10, *k8, sl1, k1, sl2, k2, sl2, k1, sl2, k15, [sl1, k1] 4 times, sl1, k9; rep from * two more times, k9.

Row 25: With Rainforest, k10, *[sl2, k1] 2 times, sl1, k5, sl2, k9, sl1, [k1, sl2] 3 times, sl1, k11, sl3, k1, sl2, k1; rep from * two more times, k9.

Row 27: With Serene, k10, *k7, sl1, k1, sl2, k3, [sl1, k1] 4 times, sl1, k11, sl2, k1, sl2, k2, sl2, k1, sl1, k7; rep from * two more times, k9.

Row 29: With Rainforest, k10, *[sl2, k1] 2 times, sl1, k4, sl3, k11, sl2, k1, sl2, k9, sl2, k5, [sl2, k1] 2 times; rep from * two more times, k9.

Row 31: With Serene, k10, *k7, sl2, k1, sl1, k3, sl2, k1, sl2, k2, sl2, k1, sl1, k5, [sl1, k1] 4 times, sl1, k3, sl2, k1, sl1, k6; rep from * two more times, k9.

Row 33: With Rainforest, k10, *[sl2, k1] 2 times, sl1, k4, sl3, k5, sl2, k5, sl2, k11, sl3, k4, [sl2, k1] 2 times; rep from * two more times, k9.

Row 35: With Serene, k10, *k8, sl2, k4, [sl1, k1] 2 times, sl1, k3, sl2, k1, sl1, k2, sl1, k1, sl2, k2, sl2, k1, sl2, k3, sl1, k1, sl2, k6; rep from * two more times, k9.

Row 37: With Rainforest, k10, *k2, sl3, k1, sl2, k2, sl2, k7, sl3, k4, sl1, k5, sl2, k5, sl3, k4, sl1, k5; rep from * two more times, k9.

Row 39: With Serene, k10, *k1, sl1, k10, sl1, k1, sl2, k1, sl2, k3, sl1, k1, sl2, k1, sl1, k2, sl3, [sl1, k1] 2 times, sl1, k4, sl2, k2, sl1, k4; rep from * two more times, k9.

Row 41: With Rainforest, k10, *k3, [sl2, k1] 2 times, sl3, k1, sl1, k7, sl1, k4, sl1, k4, sl3, k5, sl4, k2, sl1, k6; rep from * two more times, k9.

Row 43: With Serene, k10, *k2, sl1, k9, [sl1, k1] 5 times, k1, sl2, k2, sl2, k1, sl1, k3, sl2, k1, sl2, k7, sl1, k5; rep from * two more times, k9.

Row 45: With Rainforest, k10, *k5, sl3, k1, sl2, k2, sl1, k5, [sl1, k2] 2 times, sl2, k4, sl3, k5, sl2, k1, sl3, k7; rep from * two more times, k9.

Row 47: With Serene, k10, *k4, sl1, k6, sl1, k2, sl2, k1, sl2, k2, sl1, k6, sl2, k4, [sl1, k1] 2 times, [sl1, k6] 2 times; rep from * two more times, k9.

Row 49: With Rainforest, k10, *k6, sl4, k2, sl2, k5, sl1, [k3, sl4] 2 times, k5, sl3, k10; rep from * two more times, k9.

Row 51: With Serene, k10, *k5, [sl1, k4] 2 times, sl1, k1, sl1, k2, s1, k1, sl1, k4, sl1, k6, sl2, k1, sl2, k3, sl1, k9; rep from * two more times, k9.

Row 53: With Rainforest, k10, *k7, sl1, k5, sl2, k3, sl1, k5, sl3, k3, sl4, k5, sl1, k12; rep from * two more times, k9.

Row 55: With Serene, k10, *k6, sl1, k1, sl1, k3, sl1, k6, sl1, k3, sl1, k3, sl1, k1, sl1, k5, sl1, k1, sl1, k2, sl1, k11; rep from * two more times, k9.

Row 57: With Rainforest, k10, *k14, sl3, k8, sl1, k5, sl4, k3, sl1, k13; rep from * two more times, k9.

Row 59: With Serene, k10, *k7, sl1, k5, sl1, k3, sl1, k6, sl1, k1, sl1, k3, sl1, k8, sl1, k12; rep from * two more times, k9.

Row 61: With Rainforest, k10, *k15, sl1, k17, sl2, k1, sl2, k14; rep from * two more times, k9.

Row 63: With Serene, k10, *k14, sl1, k1, sl1, k8, sl1, k6, sl1, k5, sl1, k13; rep from * two more times, k9.

Row 65: With Rainforest, k10, *k35, sl1, k16; rep from * two more times, k9.

Row 67: With Serene, k10, *k15, sl1, k18, sl1, k1, sl1, k15; rep from * two more times, k9.

Row 69: With Rainforest, k all sts.

Row 71: With Serene, as Row 65.

Row 73: With Rainforest, k all sts.

Row 75: With Serene, k all sts.

Rep Rows 1-76 five more times.

CHART INSTRUCTIONS

Row 1 (RS): With Rainforest, k9, work Row 1 of the chart, working the repeat section a total of three times, k9.

Row 2 and all WS rows: K the same sts as k in previous row, with the active color; and slip all of the same slipped sts as slipped in previous row, wyif.

Continue working from the chart as set, for another 74 rows, to complete the chart.

Rep Rows 1-76 five more times.

FINISHING

Change to 5.5mm needles.

Cast off sts using a knitted cast off (see Techniques: Knitted Cast Off) or a cast off of your choice.

Weave in all ends and steam block. The blanket is very stretchy and won't change significantly, but a gentle blocking will help to straighten the stitches.

Serene

Rainforest

Pattern Repeat

TIP

If you find that you knit mosaic motifs much tighter than when you work garter stitch I recommend switching to your smaller needles (5.5mm) on Row 61 and then switch back to your larger needles (6mm) when you finish all rows in the motif. Rows 61-76 have only a few slipped stitches which can impact your gauge (tension) from the earlier rows in the motif.

103

Alternative Colorway

Yarn

Lion Brand 24/7 Cotton Yarn (100% mercerized cotton), worsted, 100g (170m/186yds), in the following shades:

- Creamsicle (132EF)
- Beets (146AM)

Needles

- 4.5mm (US 7) needles
- 5mm (US 8) needles

Gauge (tension)

21 sts and 42 rows measures 10 x 10cm (4 x 4in) over mosaic motif using 5mm needles.

One of my favorite things to knit with a new motif or stitch pattern is to make a quick dishcloth. This is a great way to practice your new stitch and at the end you have a functional project instead of a swatch that likely will sit in your knitting pile for years to come. Lion Brand 24/7 Cotton has a great selection of colors to make fun dishcloths – I chose Creamsicle and Beets and made one repeat of the motif with the Creamsicle Saguaros and then swapped the colorways on the next repeat. It's amazing how different the motifs look despite using the same colors – I love the results!

Sunday
MORNING
BLANKET

Early Sunday mornings are made for hot coffee, a good book, and if you have little ones like myself, lots of snuggles! This oversized blanket is warm enough for even the chilliest winter mornings, and is adorned with bold mosaic motifs, and vibrant colors. Play around with your color choice – unconventional colors can be fun and surprising to play with!

You Will Need

YARN

Lion Brand Wool Ease Thick & Quick Bonus Bundle (80% acrylic, 20% wool), super bulky, 340g (194m/212yds) in the following shade:

• Fisherman (099); 4 balls

Lion Brand Wool Ease Thick & Quick (80% acrylic, 20% wool), super bulky, 170g (97m/106yds), in the following shades:

• Black (153); 2 balls
• Raspberry (112); 1 ball
• Lollipop (191); 1 ball

KNITTING NEEDLES

• 9mm (US 13) needles
• 10mm (US 15) needles

Note: This pattern will be very difficult to work on straight needles, I recommend using long circular needles (the sample was knit using 116cm (45in) circular needles).

OTHER TOOLS AND MATERIALS

• Stitch markers (optional)

GAUGE (TENSION)

9 sts and 15 rows measure 10 x 10cm (4 x 4in) over stockinette mosaic motif using 10mm (US 15) needles.

FINISHED SIZE

127 x 147cm (50 x 58in) after blocking

Pattern Notes

The blanket is worked flat in a rectangle in stockinette stitch, then the sides are picked up and worked in garter stitch.

This pattern switches colors frequently; feel free to carry your colors up the side, or break the yarn as you see fit. For my sample, I maintained Fisherman throughout, and then broke each additional color after each motif – this prevented the leading edge from getting tight.

On all right side rows, slip all of the slipped stitches with yarn in back.

On all wrong side rows, slip all of the slipped stitches with yarn in front.

If you would like to change the sizing of this pattern, cast on a multiple of 24+6 sts. For example, 24x4=96. 96+6=102 cast on stitches.

Chart Notes

Each square represents a stitch. The chart begins at the lower right corner on Row 1.

Only RS (odd numbered) rows are charted and are read from right to left.

The color of the first stitch in the chart always determines the active color used for the next two rows.

PATTERN

SET-UP

Using 9mm needles and Fisherman, cast on 102 sts using a long tail cast on.

Knit all stitches for 13 rows, ending after a WS row (garter stitch).

Change to 10mm needles.

SECTION 1: STRIPES WITH SINGLE SLIPPED STITCH

Row 1 (RS): Using Fisherman, k all sts.

Row 2: Using Fisherman, p all sts.

Row 3: Using Raspberry, k all sts.

Row 4: Using Raspberry, p all sts.

Rows 5 to 6: Rep Rows 1-2.

Row 7: Using Black, [k1, sl1] rep to 2 st remaining, k2.

Row 8: Using Black, p1, [p1, sl1] rep to 1 st remaining, p1.

Rows 9 to 14: Rep Rows 1-6.

SECTION 2: MOSAIC MOTIF A

Follow either the written instructions or the charted instructions below.

If you wish to use markers for the repeats, place a marker after the second stitch, and then every 24 sts to the final four stitches.

WRITTEN INSTRUCTIONS

Row 1 (RS): With Black, k2, *sl1, k1, sl3, k17, sl2; rep from * three more times, sl1, k1, sl1, k1.

Row 2 and all WS rows: P the same sts as k in previous row, with the active color; and slip all of the same slipped sts as slipped in previous row, wyif.

Row 3: With Fisherman, k2, *k1, sl1, k3, [sl1, k1] 9 times, k1; rep from * three more times, k1, sl1, k2.

Row 5: With Black, k2, *k4, [sl1, k1] 10 times; rep from * three more times, k4.

Row 7: With Fisherman, k2, *[k3, sl1] 2 times, [k1, sl1] 6 times, k3, sl1; rep from * three more times, k4.

Row 9: With Black, k2, *sl1, k1, sl1, k3, [sl1, k1] 7 times, sl1, k3; rep from * three more times, [sl1, k1] 2 times.

Row 11: With Fisherman, k2, *k1, [sl1, k3] 2 times, [sl1, k1] 5 times, k2, sl1, k2; rep from * three more times, k1, sl1, k2.

Row 13: With Black, k2, *[sl1, k1] 3 times, k2, [sl1, k1] 5 times, sl1, k3, sl1, k1; rep from * three more times, [sl1, k1] 2 times.

Row 15: With Fisherman, k2, *[k1, sl1] 2 times, [k3, sl1] 2 times, [k1, sl1] 2 times, [k3, sl1] 2 times; rep from * three more times, k1, sl1, k2.

Row 17: With Black, k2, *[sl1, k1] 4 times, k2, [sl1, k1] 4 times, k2, [sl1, k1] 2 times; rep from * three more times, [sl1, k1] 2 times.

Row 19: With Fisherman, k2, *[k1, sl1] 3 times, [k3, sl1] 4 times, k1, sl1; rep from * three more times, k1, sl1, k2.

Row 21: With Black, k2, *[sl1, k1] 5 times, k2, sl1, k1, sl1, k3, [sl1, k1] 3 times; rep from * three more times, [sl1, k1] 2 times.

Row 23: With Fisherman, k2, *[k1, sl1] 4 times, [k3, sl1] 3 times, [k1, sl1] 2 times; rep from * three more times, k1, sl1, k2.

Row 25: With Black, k2, *[sl1, k1] 6 times, k4, [sl1, k1] 4 times; rep from * three more times, [sl1, k1] 2 times.

Row 27: With Fisherman, k2, *[k1, sl1] 5 times, [k3, sl1] 2 times, [sl1, k1] 3 times; rep from * three more times, k1, sl1, k2.

Row 29: With Black, k2, *k10, sl3, k1, s3, k7; rep from * three more times, k4.

CHART INSTRUCTIONS

Row 1 (RS): With Black, work Row 1 of Mosaic Motif A Chart, working repeat section four times.

Row 2 and all WS rows: P the same sts as k in previous row, with the active color; and slip all of the same slipped sts as slipped in previous row, wyif.

Continue working from the chart as set, for another 28 rows, to complete the chart.

SECTION 3: STRIPES WITH SINGLE SLIPPED STITCH

Rep Section 1: Stripes with Single Slipped Stitch.

SECTION 4: MOSAIC MOTIF B

Follow either the written instructions or the charted instructions below. If you wish to use markers for the repeats, place a marker after the first stitch, and then every 24 sts to the final five stitches.

WRITTEN INSTRUCTIONS

Row 1 (RS): With Lollipop, k1, *sl1, k3, sl2, k1, sl2, [k3, sl1] 2 times, sl1, k1, sl2, k3; rep from * three more times, sl1, k4.

Row 2 and all WS rows: P the same sts as k in previous row, with the active color; and slip all of the same slipped sts as slipped in previous row, wyif.

Row 3: With Fisherman, k1, *[k1, sl1] 2 times, k5, [sl1, k1] 3 times, sl1, k5, sl1, k1, sl1; rep from * three more times, [k1, sl1] 2 times, k1.

MOSAIC MOTIF A

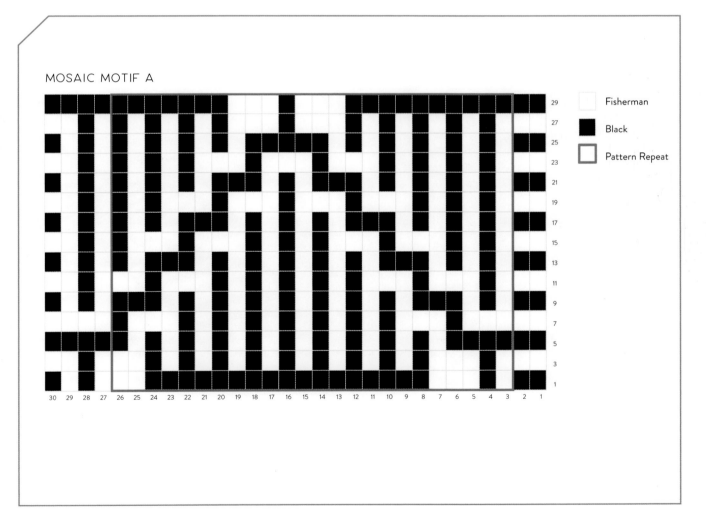

	Fisherman
■	Black
☐	Pattern Repeat

Row 5: With Lollipop, k1, *[sl1, k11] 2 times; rep from * three more times, sl1, k4.

Row 7: With Fisherman, k1, *k3, [sl1, k5] 3 times, sl1, k2, rep from * three more times, k3, sl1, k1.

Row 9: With Lollipop, k1, *k6, sl1, k11, sl1, k5; rep from * three more times, k5.

Row 11: With Fisherman, k1, *k3, [sl1, k1] 4 times, k4, [sl1, k1] 3 times, sl1, k2; rep from * three more times, k3, sl1, k1.

Row 13: With Lollipop, k1, *k1, sl2, k3, sl1, k3, sl2, k1, sl2, k3, sl1, k3, sl2; rep from * three more times, k1, sl2, k2.

CHART INSTRUCTIONS

Row 1 (RS): With Lollipop, work Row 1 of Mosaic Motif B chart, working repeat section four times.

Row 2 and all WS rows: P the same sts as k in previous row, with the active color; and slip all of the same slipped sts as slipped in previous row, wyif.

Continue working from the chart as set, for another 12 rows, to complete the chart.

NEXT STEPS

Rep Sections 1-4 one more time.

Rep Sections 1-3 one more time.

Change to 9mm needles.

With Fisherman, knit all stitches for 13 rows (garter stitch).

Cast off sts using an Icelandic cast off (see Techniques: Icelandic Cast Off) or a cast off of your choice.

BORDER

Using Fisherman and 9mm needles, pick up and knit approximately 130 sts evenly across one of the long edges of the blanket. To do so, pick up two stitches for every three rows, and occasionally one stitch for every two rows (see Techniques: Picking Up Stitches).

Knit in garter stitch for 11 rows, ending after a WS row.

Cast off sts using an Icelandic cast off (see Techniques: Icelandic Cast Off) or a cast off of your choice.

Repeat the garter stitch border on the remaining long edge of the blanket.

FINISHING

Weave in all ends, and block as desired. For a blanket this size, I found it easiest to run the blanket through a gentle cycle in my washing machine, and then spread it out on a series of towels on the floor to absorb excess water. The blanket is very stretchy and won't change significantly, but a gentle blocking will help to straighten the stitches.

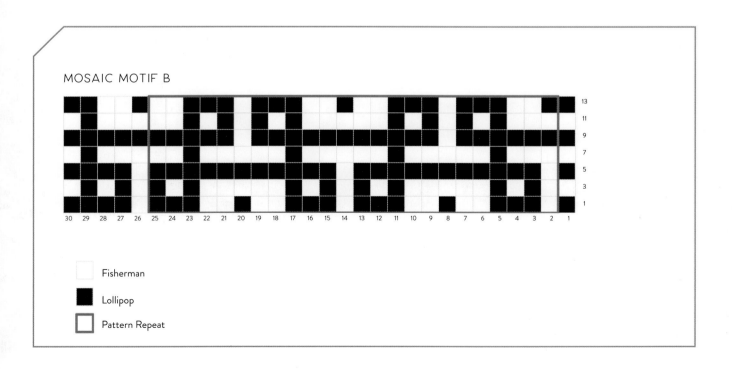

MOSAIC MOTIF B

13 11 9 7 5 3 1

30 29 28 27 26 25 24 23 22 21 20 19 18 17 16 15 14 13 12 11 10 9 8 7 6 5 4 3 2 1

☐ Fisherman

■ Lollipop

☐ Pattern Repeat

Alternative Colorway

Yarn

Lion Brand Wool Ease Thick & Quick (80% acrylic, 20% wool), super bulky, 170g (97m/106yds), in the following shades:

- Night Shadow (540B)
- Deep Lagoon (623D)
- Arctic Ice (648D)

Needles

Same as pattern.

Gauge (tension)

Same as pattern.

I wanted to play around with a tri-color version of my Sunday Morning Blanket, so I chose Wool Ease Thick & Quick in three moody, cool shades: Night Shadow, Deep Lagoon, and Arctic Ice and removed the horizontal stripes from the pattern. I love how the variegated shades make a more rustic version of this afghan.

Also, if you aren't a fan of picking up stitches along the side, you can cast on a couple of extra stitches (I would add at least five) at the beginning and end of each row and work them in garter stitch. This helps to remove any curling that might happen with the stockinette stitch nature of this pattern.

TECHNIQUES

Learning to knit can be intimidating – but remember every knitter started with the basics at one time. There are hundreds of knitting stitches and techniques used in patterns all over the world. But, luckily, you don't need to learn all of these to master the patterns in this book! Here is a helpful guide to all the techniques introduced throughout this book.

Knitting Skills

ABBREVIATIONS

The patterns in this book use the basic knitting abbreviations listed below.

k - knit

kfb - knit into the front and back of one stitch

k2tog - knit two stitches together

m1r - make one right leaning stitch

p - purl

pm - place marker

rep - repeat

RS - right side

sl - slip stitch purlwise

sm - slip marker

st(s) - stitches

tbl - through the back loop

wyif - with the yarn in front

WS - wrong side

All the patterns in this book use repeated sections of instructions to produce the mosaic motifs. Repeated sequences are indicated as follows:

*...; rep from * to, work instructions from * to; and then repeat that section up to the point specified

*...; rep from * one/two/three more times, work the instructions from * to; and then repeat that section the number of times specified

[....]once/twice/3 times, work the instructions between the square brackets the total number of times specified

If you are looking for help with your knit stitch, your cast off, or wondering how to weave a mattress stitch, you've come to the right place!

LONG TAIL CAST ON

The long tail cast on is my favorite cast on – it's the first cast on that most knitters learn, it's fast, stretchy, and versatile!

1. Create a slip knot on your right needle with a tail that is at least four times as wide as your project (be generous...it is very frustrating to run out of tail right before you cast on the correct number of stitches). Hold the slip knot with your right hand.

2. With your left hand, insert your index finger and thumb between the two strands. Next, using your remaining three fingers, grip the hanging strands firmly. **(1)**

3. With slight tension on the yarn, insert the needle under the strand that is wrapped around your thumb. **(2)**

4. With the lifted strand on the needle, go over the upper strand that is on the index finger. Lift this strand up with the needle. **(3)**

5. Bring the strand through the opening that is near the thumb. Remove thumb from the strand.

6. Pull down on both strands until the stitch is on the needle. **(4)**

7. Repeat Steps 3-6 for each stitch that needs to be cast on.

TIP

If you find that your long tail cast on is too tight, go up a needle size when you cast on, and then go back to your planned needle size on the first row.

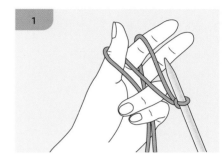

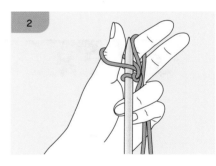

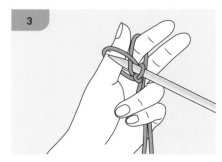

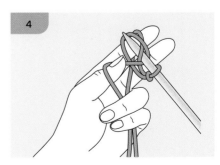

KNIT STITCH

1. Hold the needle with the cast on stitches in your left hand. Hold the working needle in your right hand, with the yarn loosely wrapped around your fingers. Insert the right needle from the front to the back into the first cast on stitch on the left needle. Keep the yarn at the back and the right needle under the left needle. **(1)**

2. Wrap the yarn under and over the right needle clockwise. **(2)**

3. With the right needle, catch the wrapped yarn and pull it through the cast on stitch. **(3)**

4. Slide the cast on stitch off the left hand needle and keep the new stitch on the right needle. **(4)** Continue these steps until all stitches have been worked on the left hand needle – this is one complete knit row.

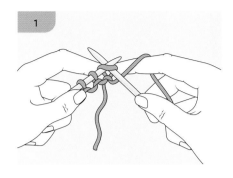
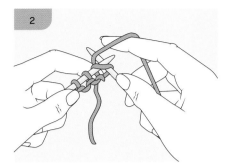
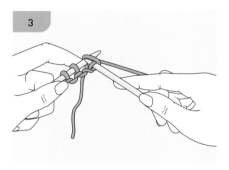
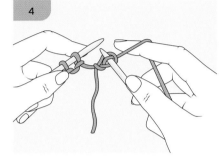

PURL STITCH

1. Hold the working needle in your right hand and the needle with the stitches in your left hand. Insert the right needle from the back to the front into the first stitch on the left hand needle. Keep the yarn at the front of the work and the right needle in front of the left needle. **(1)**

2. Wrap the yarn counterclockwise around the right hand needle. **(2)**

3. With the right needle, draw the yarn backwards through the stitch on the left hand needle, creating a loop on the right needle. **(3)**

4. Slide the stitch off the left needle and keep the new stitch on the right needle. **(4)** Continue these steps until all stitches have been worked on the left hand needle - this is one complete purl row.

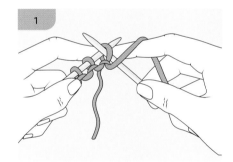
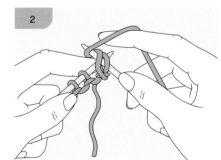
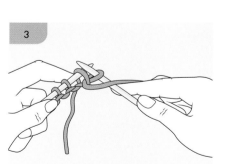
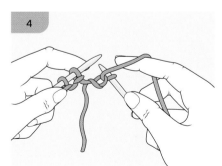

SLIP STITCH PURLWISE

Insert your right hand needle into the next stitch as if to purl, and just slide it from your left needle to your right needle without purling the stitch.

K2TOG

Insert the right hand needle from front to back into the next two stitches on the left needle. Wrap the yarn around the right needle (as if to knit) and pull it through. This will create a decrease that slants to the right and will decrease your stitch count by one stitch.

KFB

Insert the right needle knitwise into the stitch that will be increased. Wrap the yarn around the right needle and pull it through as if knitting, but leave the stitch on the left needle.

Insert the right needle into the back of the same stitch. Wrap the yarn around the needle and pull it through. Slip the stitch from the left needle – you now have two stitches on the right needle.

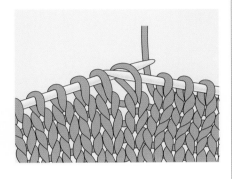
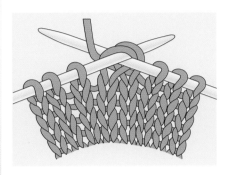
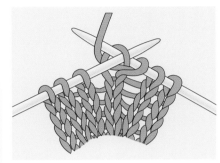

M1R

1. Insert the left needle from back to front under the horizontal strand between the last stitch worked and the next stitch on the left hand needle. **(1)**

2. Knit this stitch through the back loop. This will create a practically invisible increase between the two stitches and will slant to the right. **(2)**

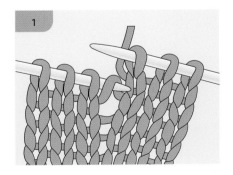
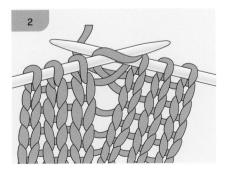

ICELANDIC CAST OFF

The Icelandic cast off is my favorite cast off when I need to cast off a project that ends in garter stitch. This method is very stretchy and nearly blends into garter stitch fabric. This technique is slightly more complicated than the basic knitted cast off, but after a couple of stitches you'll be flying through your cast off!

1. Knit one stitch, place the stitch back onto the left hand needle. **(1-2)**

2. Insert the tip of the right hand needle purlwise into the front loop of the first stitch on the left needle. Make sure the tip of the right needle is at the front of the tip of the left needle.

3. Now insert the tip of the right hand needle knitwise into the front loop of the second stitch on the left hand needle.

4. Wrap the tip of the right hand needle with the yarn and pull the wrap through the front loop of the second stitch. (In other words, knit the second stitch through the loop of the first stitch.) **(3)**

5. Slip both stitches off the left hand needle, and keep the new stitch on the right hand needle. **(4)**

6. Place the new stitch on the left hand needle. **(5)**

7. Repeat Steps 2 to 6 until you have cast off all stitches. Break yarn and pull tail through the last stitch. Pull tight to secure.

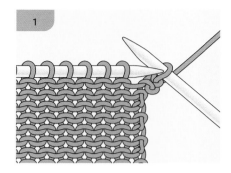

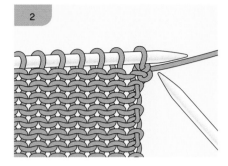

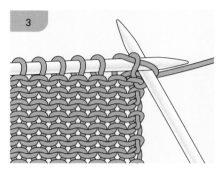

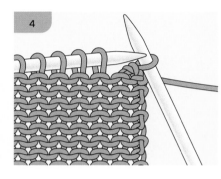

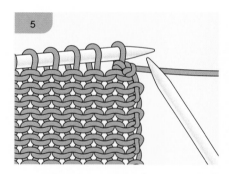

TIP

Due to the stretchy nature of the Icelandic cast off, you may find that you need to pull your stitches a bit tighter than you would for a knitted cast off in order to keep an even edge. If pulling the stitches tighter doesn't help, you can always go down a needle size when casting off.

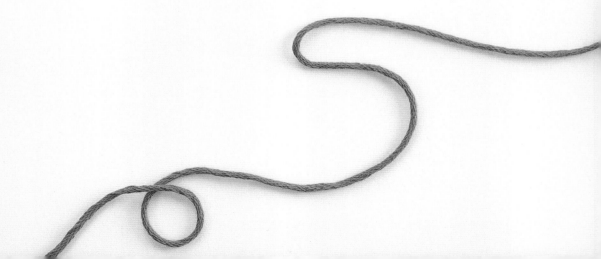

KNITTED CAST OFF

The knitted cast off is the most commonly used cast off for knitters. It creates a neat, polished edge, and has some stretchiness to it.

1. Knit the first two stitches on your knitting needle.

2. Insert your left needle into the first stitch on your right needle. **(1)**

3. Lift the first stitch over the second stitch and drop it off the needle. (1 stitch decreased.) **(2-3)**

4. Knit another stitch from the left needle (you have two stitches on your right needle again).

5. Repeat Steps 2-4 until all stitches have been knit and only one stitch remains.

6. With the last stitch on your needle, cut your yarn leaving at least a 10cm (4in) tail. Pull the tail through the final loop, and pull snug.

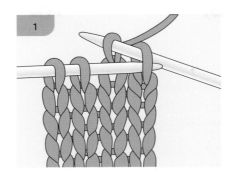

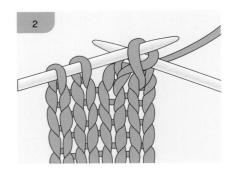

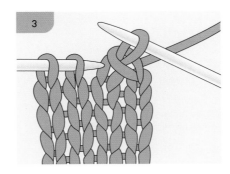

TIPS

If you tend to knit tightly, cast off with one needle size larger – this will make sure your edge isn't too tight.

If you're instructed to cast off in pattern (like on the Tundra Tamer Cowl or the Comfy Cozy Mug Cozies), you will simply cast off as in the above instructions, but instead of knitting every stitch, you will work the stitch as either a knit or a purl stitch based upon what was knit in the previous ribbed row.

PICKING UP STITCHES

Picking up stitches allows you to create a continuous fabric by knitting new stitches onto the existing ones. The exact technique for picking up the stitches depends on the type of fabric you are picking up stitches on, and what kind of fabric you'll be working on after the stitches are picked up. The instructions here are for how to pick up stitches on the edge of stockinette stitch and then creating garter stitch fabric (as seen in the Sunday Morning Blanket).

Because of the difference in gauge (tension) between rows and stitches (there are typically fewer stitches in 10cm (4in) than there are rows), the general rule of thumb is to pick up two stitches for every three rows (i.e. pick up, pick up, skip).

To pick up stitches, you will need a set of needles and the yarn you'll be working with (sometimes I hold a smaller sized needle in my left hand to more easily pick up the desired stitches).

1. Hold your work with the right side facing you and the edge you are picking up stitches from horizontally in front of you.

2. If picking up stitches along the cast on or cast off edge **(1)**, insert the right hand needle between the cast off edge and the previous row from the front to the back. If working along the side of the project, insert the needle from the front to the back in the space between the first and second stitches.

3. Wrap the right hand needle with the working yarn as if to knit **(2)**. Pull the yarn through to complete the stitch.

4. Repeat Steps 2-3 along the edge of the project until all stitches have been picked up.

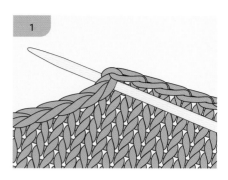

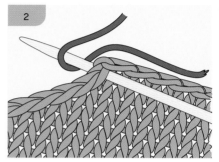

MATTRESS STITCH

Mattress stitch seams together two knitted pieces with an invisible vertical join. It can join together both stockinette and ribbed edges. This makes your project appear as though you knit in the round, even though your project was made flat.

The mattress stitch will create a noticeable ridge on the wrong side of your work, but it isn't visible on the right side of your work. Use a yarn color that is the same as the one that you used on your project to make the seam even more invisible.

Note: You lose one stitch from ether edge to the seam, so often the selvedge edge on mosaic motifs will disappear, creating a beautiful seamless look. This is also why patterns with ribbing that are seamed together have a stitch count of a multiple of 4+2 to account for the stitches that disappear when seamed together.

1. Thread a piece of yarn (this can be your cast on/cast off tail, or an entirely new piece of yarn) onto a tapestry needle. You will need yarn that is at least twice as long as the length of your seam.

2. Lay the two edges that you want to seam side by side with the right side facing you.

3. Identify the first two columns of stitches on the right piece, and slide your needle through the first bar between the two knit stitches. This bar looks like a ladder between the "V's" of the first two knit stitches. Pull the tapestry needle through. If you're using a separate piece of yarn, leave a tail at least 10cm (4in) long for weaving in at the end.

4. Slide your needle underneath the first bar between the first two stitches on the left piece.

5. Draw the needle through the next bar on the right piece. This will be the next "rung" of the "ladder" that you went through in Step 3.

6. Go back to the left piece and draw the yarn underneath the bar above the bar in Step 4.

7. Repeat steps 5-6 along the entire length of the desired seam. Every couple of stitches, tug on the yarn gently to close the seam. (Note: If your seam puckers, you pulled it too tight! Gently stretch it out before you continue seaming.)

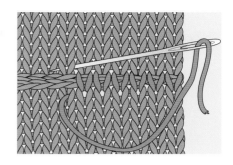

Finishing Your Work

There are so many ways to finish your project! I highly recommend blocking your knits, no matter how it'll be used. But, beyond that, finishing is up to you. I've included instructions on how to add fringe and tassels – you can add these fun design elements to any pattern in this book

BLOCKING

Blocking is easy and can even be fun. I highly recommend blocking any project you complete (aside from a dishcloth if you're going to use it right away!). Blocking helps to shape your knitting and makes your stitches smooth and look much neater. I like to block my knitting before I weave in my edges or seam pieces together.

Natural Fibers

Yarn that is mostly natural fibers (wool, cotton, bamboo, etc) will block easily by using the soaking method.

1. Soak the project in cool water that has a small drop of gentle soap (they make wool-specific soap, but I've found that my daughter's baby shampoo works just fine).

2. Lay the project out on a towel or a foam mat that will allow you to pin and shape the project as desired.

3. Let your art dry (for a few hours, or a couple of days depending on the size of the project, temperature, and humidity), and your piece is blocked!

Acrylic Yarn

I've heard many knitters say that you don't need to block acrylic yarn. I've heard others say that you can't block acrylic. I'm here to tell you that that is absolutely not true: Blocking will transform the look of your projectsbut you must take a different approach when blocking an acrylic yarn project.

All you need is a garment steamer or an iron with a steam setting, your foam blocking boards (or children's foam play mats), straight pins, and a tape measure.

1. Lay your project out on the blocking boards, and begin pinning it to the measurements that the pattern specified. Use as many pins as you need to get your project the exact shape you desire.

2. Steam block the fabric by simply hovering the garment steamer or the iron on steam setting about 1.2cm (½in) above it. Continuously move back and forth over the project so the entire piece becomes damp and softens up a bit. Be very careful to not touch the fabric with the iron – IT WILL MELT THE YARN – we'll all cry, and we can't have that happening.

3. Allow your knitting to dry and voila – you've blocked acrylic yarn!

ADDING FRINGE

To make fringe, all you need are your yarn, a pair of scissors, a crochet hook, and a piece of cardboard. Cut your cardboard to be about at least 20cm (8in) long and 1.2cm (½in) wider than the length of your finished fringe (i.e. if your fringe is going to be 10cm (4 in) long, cut your cardboard to be about 12cm (4½in) wide.

1. Wind your yarn around your piece of cardboard widthwise. To ensure all the fringe is approximately the same length, don't pile the yarn in one area on the board, rather wrap the yarn around the cardboard in a uniform layer across the entire width.

2. Cut your yarn along one edge of the cardboard so that your cut yarn will be twice the length of your fringe.

3. To attach the fringe, take a piece of fringe (or multiple pieces if desired), and fold it in half lengthwise.

4. Working from the back of your knitting, insert the crochet hook into the spot where you want to place fringe.

5. Grab your loop of yarn with the crochet hook from the front side of the knitting. Pull the loop through the fabric to the back side.

6. Lift the loop and pull the ends of the yarn through. Pull the loop tight.

7. Repeat Steps 3-6 until all fringing has been attached.

8. After all fringing has been attached, trim your fringe tassels to a uniform length. If desired, you can steam block the fringe.

CREATING TASSELS

Tassels are easy! All you need is yarn, a pair of scissors, a tapestry needle, and a piece of cardboard. Cut your cardboard to be about at least 20cm (8in) long and 1.2cm (½in) wider than the length of your finished tassel (i.e. if your tassel is going to be 10cm (4in) long, cut your cardboard to be about 12cm (4½in) wide.

1. Wind your yarn around your piece of cardboard widthwise (add a few more wraps than you think you'll need!). To ensure the yarn in the tassel is approximately the same length, don't pile the yarn in one area on the board, rather wrap the yarn around the cardboard in a uniform layer across the entire width.

2. Cut your yarn along one edge of the cardboard so that your cut yarn will be twice the length of your tassel.

3. Cut a piece of yarn approximately 38cm (15in) in length. Wrap this piece around the middle of the cut yarn and tie a secure knot. This will be the top of your tassel, and the ends will be used to secure the tassel to your knitting.

4. Cut another piece of yarn, approximately 25cm (10in) long and wrap it around the body of the tassel, approximately 2.5cm (1in) from the top of the tassel.

5. Tie a secure knot and wrap the tails around the tassel several times to make the "head" of the tassel more defined.

6. Using the tapestry needle, pull the ends through the center of the tassel.

7. Give your tassel a trim so the ends are uniform.

8. Using the tails on the top of the tassel, and the tapestry needle, secure the tassel to your knitting, weaving in ends as necessary.

Designing Your Own Motifs

Now that you've worked on a few mosaic knitting projects, do you have an itch to try your own design? It's fun! There are two ground rules I like to follow when designing a motif, we'll go over those now, and then you'll find graph paper so you can try your hand at making your own chart or two!

TIP

Designing a mosaic motif using just written instructions is very difficult; start by charting/sketching out what you want the motif to look like, and then you can create written instructions if you so desire.

THE GROUND RULES

- The first and last stitch of every chart (sometimes called the selvedge stitches) indicate the "active" color of each row. Alternate your active color every two rows.
- Keep the floats short.
- One of the best parts of mosaic motifs is that there are no long, fiddly floats on the WS. However, this can only be accomplished by switching colors frequently.
- When designing, keep the runs of your inactive color to less than five stitches (I usually stick to less than three stitches, but I sometimes break this rule!).
- This means that in a "black" row of a chart, have no more than three consecutive white stitches.
- In a "white" row of a chart, have no more than three consecutive black stitches.
- Sometimes long color runs are easy to miss on the edges of the repeat section of a chart, so do a quick count of how many stitches you have at the beginning/end of your repeat section in each color as you're designing.
- Mosaic motifs work best with geometric rather than organic shapes.
- Mosaic motifs tend toward geometric shapes because you can only slip a stitch of the opposite color if it lies immediately below the stitch you want to slip – unlike in stranded knitting, a color can only appear in a row if it is the active color, or if there is a stitch of the same color to pull up from below.
- This might sound simple, but as soon as you start playing around with charts you will see how this can limit what your designs might look like.

Let's see a visual:

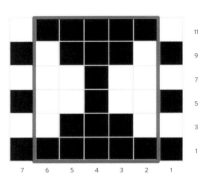

Chart 1

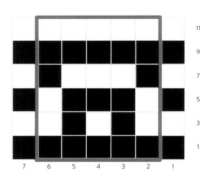

Chart 2

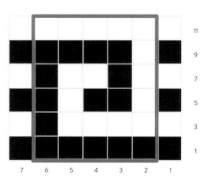

Chart 3

Chart 1 won't work because Rows 5, 9, and 11 all have stitches in the inactive color that weren't in the previous row. Plus, Row 11 has only stitches in the inactive color aside from the selvedge edges – this is impossible. Chart 2 is better, but still won't work because Row 7 has two black stitches that were white in the previous row. Tricky, right? Black stitches are always introduced in rows that have a black stitch in the first row, and vice versa with the white stitches.

The easiest way to learn these rules is to practice! The graph paper layout provided will enable you to practice making your own charts. I included row/stitch numbering, but feel free to ignore the numbering and start your chart anywhere you want on the page. You can likely fit a few draft charts on the page, and if you want to make even more charts, make a copy of the page or find a piece of graph paper, or there are many free charting software programs online (I used Stitch Fiddle for all the charts you find in this book).

Start with simple motifs, and then let your imagination free! Have yarn and needles on standby so you can see what your motif looks like in real life – sometimes the most simple motif repeated several times can have stunning results!

About the Author

Ashleigh Wempe is a self-taught knitter and independent knitting pattern designer who loves to experiment with colorwork. She is a proud Air Force veteran with a day job as a Process Engineer. Born and raised in the Midwest, Ashleigh recently returned to her Minnesota hometown after spending the last 15 years residing and traveling throughout Latin America, the USA, and Korea. This is her first book and she looks forward to making many more! Ashleigh's designs have been featured in several publications and are available on Ravelry. She lives with her husband and two firecracker daughters who are forever unraveling her yarn and hiding her stitch markers!

You can find her online at AshleighWempe.com and on Instagram @AshleighWempe or on Ravelry.

Suppliers

I am beyond thankful to Lion Brand who offered yarn support for the vast majority of the patterns in this book. I chose to use Lion Brand exclusively because of their affordability and accessibility to most knitters – plus, every yarn you will find in this book is machine washable! I wanted to create a book full of easily giftable patterns – and in my experience it's almost always a good idea to gift washable rather than hand-wash only gifts.

Lion Brand

Address: 135 Kero Road, Carlstadt, NJ, 07072 USA

Email: support@lionbrand.com

Phone: 1-800-661-7551

Acknowledgements

Just like raising kids, it takes a village to write a book! This process has been an incredible journey and it wouldn't have been possible without the following people.

To my editor, Sarah Callard, thank you for trusting me with this undertaking and always being there to answer a question along the way. Thank you to the rest of the staff at David and Charles for accepting my proposal, and helping to make this book a reality!

To my technical editor, Sam Winkler, from Bewildered Panda Knits, thank you so much for going over my patterns with a fine-tooth comb – you have a true eye for detail!

Thank you to Katrina Moyer for doing my hair and makeup for my author photo – you helped a girl who never wears makeup feel natural and beautiful! And thank you to Bre from Page Family Photography for making a quick photo shoot easy and relaxing!

A larger than life thank you to Lion Brand Yarns for generously providing yarn support for the vast majority of the patterns in this book.

Thank you to my parents, my sisters, and my grandparents for bravely wearing my earliest knitwear creations!

Thank you to Sophia and Olivia, my baby girls, for your never-ending love and early morning snuggles. Now that this book is complete, I can finally make all the stuffed animals and accessories you've been begging for!

Most of all, thank you to my husband, Ryan, for being my sounding board, my voice of reason, always filling up my cup of coffee, taking the girls to the park, editing the non-knitting parts of this book, and overall making this book happen! It wouldn't have been possible without you! I love you!

Index